Advancing the Ministries of the Gospel

AMG *Publishers*

God's Word to you is our highest calling.

PREPARING MY HEART *for*

EASTER

A Woman's Journey to the Cross and Beyond

Ann Marie Stewart

Dedicated to
my parents:
Bill and Ruth Roetcisoender
who celebrate life and look forward to an eternity with Jesus

Preparing My Heart for Easter:
A Woman's Journey to the Cross and Beyond

© 2006 by Ann M. Stewart

Published by AMG Publishers. All Rights Reserved.

First Printing, 2006

ISBN 10: 0-89957-053-4

ISBN 13: 978-089957053-2

Unless otherwise noted, scripture verses are taken from the Holy Bible, New International Version, copyright 1973, 1978, 1984, International Bible Society. Used by permission of Zondervan Publishing House.

Scripture quotations marked (NASB) are from the *New American Standard Bible®*. Copyright © 1960, 1962, 1963, 1968, 1971, 1972, 1973, 1975, 1977 by The Lockman Foundation. Used by permission. (http://www.Lockman.org)

Scripture quotations marked (KJV) are from the King James Version, which is in the public domain.

Cover design by Daryle Beam at Market Street Design, Chattanooga, TN

Interior design and typesetting by PerfecType, Nashville, TN

Editing by Linda Gilden and Rick Steele

Printed in the United States of America

10 09 08 07 –W– 6 5 4 3 2

Acknowledgments

My heart is prepared to thank my friends and family. Thank you, Dad and Mom (Bill and Ruth Roetcisoender), for your continued support. I also thank Veronica Hall, who led a Bible study group and helped write the Guide for Leaders. A huge hug goes to the women who "test drove" an early model at Leesburg United Methodist Church: Kim Domin, Donna Fincher, Paulette Almond, Patti Henry, Shirley Bailey, Sarah Glaum, Marci Andrews, Kathi Pierce, Mary Frances Townsend, Jannine Vaughn; and to the women of the Edmonds, Washington test drive: Veronica Hall, Jennifer Sorensen, Michelle Hundthoft, Diana Young, Janet Wilkie, Joan Lundquist, Sherri Hamilton, Char Jacobson, and Beverly Heller. I thank on-line students Anne Miller, Nancy Fisler, Jodie Musgrove, Carrie Leslie, and Fern Tully; and heartfelt thanks go to the women at the Purcellville Baptist Women's Retreat, who gave my writing an audience.

For their faithful encouragement and prayers thanks go to Holly G. Coe, Carrie Leslie, Lydia and Milt Harris, Glenn and Helen Garner, Jane Eskew, Jill Dye, Leslie Williams, Barbara Boughton, Jodie Musgrove, Kim Domin, Marci Andrews, Joan McClenny, Anne Miller, Rachelle Knight, and Karen van der Riet.

For generous editing assistance I thank Lydia Harris and Mary Kate White, and for their spiritual proofreading, Pastor Mike Emerson, and Rick Howe, Director of Dayspring Center for Christian Studies. For graphic and technical help thanks go to Sherrill Kraakmo, and Jannine Vaughn.

Thanks to AMG editors who believe in preparing hearts for holy days.

Much love goes to a neglected husband who put up with late night editing and extra kisses go to my two daughters who endured Mommy glued to the computer.

Most of all PRAISE BE to the One who made Easter a celebration!

About the Author

ANN MARIE STEWART is the author of *Preparing My Heart for Advent: A Spiritual Pilgrimage for the Christmas Season,* and writes a bi-monthly column titled *"Ann's Lovin' Ewe"* for The Country Register. She is currently completing her first novel.

Ann's twelve years of teaching music and English prepare her to present a study that is easy to follow. While completing her Masters in Film and Television at the University of Michigan, Ann directed award-winning film and video productions.

Her expertise as a vocal soloist and choral conductor help her incorporate music into each week's lesson, while her background in acting and scriptwriting add drama to her presentation of the gospel. Ann's ultimate purpose for this book is to encourage women to meet, accept, and follow Jesus, as did so many New Testament women.

Ann and her husband, Will, and two daughters Christine and Julia run a small sheep farm in Paeonian Springs, Virginia. Ann is also an expressive and engaging speaker and singer for groups of all ages. More information can be found at **PreparingMyHeart.com** and **AMGPublishers.com.**

Introduction

A thrill went through me when I saw Him enter the city gate riding on a donkey. He was such a contrast; his faraway gaze mystified me, and yet his warm smile of acknowledgment seemed so personal. "Hosanna!" we shouted.

His disciples echoed with, "Blessed is He who comes in the Name of the Lord!"

I wasn't prepared to feel the unified surge of excitement that rippled through the crowd. Children jumped up and down to get a better look; women waved their palm branches, and men hailed him. I was engulfed in the energy, enthusiasm, and excitement of the moment. When He reached out to the children crowding around Him, He looked so much like the Sunday school pictures of my childhood.

As an actor in our community passion play, I have experienced many emotions as I seek to understand the first Easter. My various roles as follower of Christ, Mary Magdalene, and Mother of Jesus have challenged me to look at Jesus from new perspectives.

But one problem I have is that I see the resurrection backwards. I'm influenced by knowing the *end* of the story. What would it have been like to be a woman in the crowd during Jesus' day, experiencing great hope, and then great loss, not comprehending that He would return? Walt Wangerin writes in *Reliving the Passion,* that knowing the end of the story alters our experience of comprehending the final week.

> It is the experience of genuine grief that prepares for joy. . . . The disciples approached the Resurrection from their bereavement. For them the death was first, and the death was all. Easter, then, was an explosion of Newness, a marvelous splitting of heaven indeed. But for us, who return backward into the past, the Resurrection comes first, and through it we view a death which is, therefore, less consuming, less horrible, even less real. We miss the disciples' terrible, wonderful preparation." (p. 32)

How do *we* prepare ourselves for a *new* celebration of Easter? By looking at how Jesus elevated women. When I began researching *Preparing My Heart for Easter,* what struck me was the importance of *women* in the Easter story. Over and over I saw the phrase "the women" repeated.

The Women:
- traveled with Him and supported Him out of their own means (Luke 8:1–3)
- followed Him to the cross (Matthew 27:55–56; Mark 15:40–41)
- remained at the cross (Luke 23:48–49)
- saw the tomb and how His body was laid (Luke 23:55–56)
- prepared spices and returned to the tomb (Luke 24:1)
- first heard and told the Good News (Matthew 28:6–8)

- first saw the resurrected Jesus (Matthew 28:9; Mark 16:9)
- helped form the early church (Acts 1:14)

As I studied those scriptures, I had to ask, *Why were the women so devoted? Why were the women at every step of the journey?*

Discover the answers to these questions with me as we journey with Jesus and meet the women whose lives He touched. You may find yourself relating to someone whose life He changed and realize He can change your life, too. And like the women of His time, our eyes will be fixed on him as He journeys to the cross and beyond. We will join the men and women who celebrated His resurrection and see how the early church begins as our own spiritual growth develops.

To assist your study, please cut out your own bookmarks and place them in Matthew, Mark, Luke, John, Psalms, and Isaiah to help you in your reading. When multiple references are listed, the ones in parenthesis are optional scriptures for further study.

Meet Jesus in a new way this Easter season. As your relationship with Him grows, you'll never want to be without Him. Let's prepare for an Easter unlike any other, an "Explosion of Newness." Join me as we journey to Jerusalem.

Lest I forget Gethsemane, lest I forget Thine agony,
Lest I forget Thy love for me, lead me to Calvary.

"Lead Me to Calvary"
by Jennie Hussey and William Kirkpatrick

Contents

WEEK ONE:
PREPARING FOR THE JOURNEY

What Is Lent?

Monday: Packing for the Trip
Seven Weeks Before Easter

Before we journey to the cross, we'll need to pack our bags full of information. The first week of study will equip us for the following seven as we learn about AD 30, the cultural attitudes of the day toward women, and the backgrounds of Easter terms.

In *Preparing My Heart for Advent: A Spiritual Pilgrimage for the Christmas Season* (AMG Publishers, 2005), we prepared our hearts for the coming of Immanuel—*God with us*. In *Preparing My Heart for Easter* we will journey with *God with us* all the way to the cross and beyond as we learn of His death, resurrection, ascension, and the gift of the Holy Spirit.

Are you ready? You'll need your Bible, a pencil, a time and place to meet with God, and a commitment to journey with Him. The relationship you form with Jesus will *transform* your life.

Whether you're new to Bible study or a seasoned student of His Word, you will grow in wisdom as you learn about His teachings and put them into action. Right now, consider how closely you're following Him. A number of women discussed in the New Testament sought Jesus, and each forged a unique relationship with Him. Find a situation to which you can relate:

> Where will you meet with Jesus each day? What time of the day will you meet? Be deliberate in your planning and faithful to your commitment. Jesus wants a relationship with you.

I sometimes feel like the sinner woman. I cannot look into Jesus' face.

I am like the widow at Nain. I am grieving, but Jesus is seeking me.

I am like the woman at the well. I'm staying away from crowds and not seeking Jesus.

I am like Simon Peter's mother-in-law. Others bring Jesus to me.

I am like Jairus' wife. Others reveal Jesus to my family and me.

I am like the woman in the crowd listening to Jesus' lessons.
I am like Martha. I fervently serve the Lord through my actions.
I am like the woman who followed Christ. I am desperately trying to grab the fringe of His garment.
I am pleading with God like the Canaanite woman over a financial situation or a family member's health.
I know I am a sinner and have felt Jesus' forgiveness. I love to worship Him.
I am like Mary Magdalene. Jesus has so changed my life, I long to be near and serve Him.
I am like Mary, Martha's sister. I love to sit at Christ's feet

As one of these women of AD 30, what would draw you to Jesus? What was so attractive and revolutionary about Him? According to Luke 8:1–3, the women followed him from one town and village to another, supporting His ministry from their own means. As discussed in the Introduction, women play a huge role in the Easter story. Historian Paul Maier writes in *In the Fullness of Time*,

> Women play a more enviable role than men in the events of Holy Week. In contrast to the misunderstandings, betrayals, denials, and flight of the male followers of Jesus, it was women who anointed Jesus at Bethany, who punctured Peter's pretenses in the courtyard of Caiaphas, who warned Pilate to release Jesus because he was innocent, who commiserated Jesus' fate on the way to Golgotha, and who stood loyally under the cross until the end.[1]

📖 Read the passages below and note what might have caused His followers—especially women—to walk with Jesus. From each passage, list one central verse and one characteristic that might prompt you to follow Jesus. To help you in your daily study, cut out some bookmarks out of card stock or construction paper. You can use these bookmarks to mark the most frequently used books in our research.

Mark 6:30–44

_____

_____

_____

Mark 10:13–16

_____

_____

John 11:32–36

_____

_____

Matthew 18:2–5

_____

_____

Is Jesus someone you can follow? Come along for eight weeks and learn more about Him. Each day's lesson will end with practical thoughts about the truths studied so we can put Jesus' words in action.

Jesus' Words in Action: Can you weep with those who weep? Do you draw children to your lap? Do you reach out to a sad widow? Do you encourage friends whose marriages are falling apart? Do you reach out to people the world casts aside? In your actions today, how can you show the love of Jesus?

Tuesday: Tell Me the Stories of Jesus

My favorite line from the hymn "Tell Me the Story of Jesus" is "_Words full of kindness, deeds full of grace, all in the love-light of Jesus' face._" After the children in William Parker's Sunday school class begged for more stories, he gave them, as well as all of us, a story in song. Today can you sit in the "love-light of Jesus' face" and listen to His stories? What did Jesus look like to His followers? Today let's find out what attracted the crowds to Jesus.

Isaiah 53:2 says there wasn't anything handsome about Him, and New Testament scriptures seem to confirm this. Paul Maier writes,

> Jesus' physical appearance must have seemed very normal indeed—no towering figure, no nimbus, no halo. His enemies required the services of a Judas to point him out in the dusk of Jerusalem, Mary Magdalene mistook him for a gardener at the Easter

tomb, and to the Emmaus disciples he looked like nothing more than a fellow traveler. [2]

His magnetism came from within. His *words* and *actions* attracted crowds. Paul Maier also describes what He was *not* as well as what He *was*. He was *not* an ascetic, legalist, intolerant person, or wimp. He *was* a friend, a caring healer, and a man who could enjoy a party. He socialized with sinners and publicans and was strong in body, mind, and purpose.[3]

Philip Yancey, author of *The Jesus I Never Knew*, concurs with Jesus' draw and following by stating, "the Gospels present a man who has such charisma that people will sit three days straight, without food, just to hear his riveting words." He seems excitable, impulsively "moved with compassion" or "filled with pity." Yancey describes a man with a wide range of emotions: sympathy, exuberance, anger, and grief. [4] He was human and God.

> "He grew up before him like a tender shoot, and like a root out of dry ground. He had no beauty or majesty to attract us to him, nothing in his appearance that we should desire him."
> (Isaiah 53:2)

Jesus is also a great storyteller. Without a microphone, He keeps an audience of thousands riveted on a hillside. When Jesus talks to people, He engages them personally by telling stories to which all can relate. Jesus understands people and knows what they need. Let's pretend we're hearing these stories for the first time. What is it that encourages you to follow Him?

Read Luke 15.

1. What three examples does Jesus use to illustrate the joy of a sinner being found?

_____

_____

Can you see the Good Shepherd's joy at finding His single lamb? What about you, my friend? Won't He rejoice even more at knowing you are walking beside Him today? And the parable isn't even over, there's a party to celebrate the lost sheep being found. One sinner repents and Jesus reveals heaven's celebration.

But, knowing His audience, Jesus expands on the story to include a *woman* who has ten silver coins and loses one. This may equal a full day's wage. This tidy housekeeper lights a lamp, sweeps the house, and searches until the coin is found. These two stories lead into the story of the Prodigal Son. Three times Jesus shows us there is joy in heaven over the sinner who comes to know Jesus.

2. Which story could you relate to if you stood in the crowd?

_____

_____

_____

> "And when he has found it, he lays it on his shoulders, rejoicing." (Luke 15:5)

Jesus' point is clear. He wants the tax-gatherers and sinners to know, "There will be more joy in heaven over one sinner who repents, than over ninety-nine righteous persons who need no repentance" (Luke 15:7). Jesus reveals the reason He has come: to seek the lost.

That encourages me! This man loves even the lowliest. He doesn't favor kings and priests, but sinners and *nobodies*.

> *But when you give a banquet, invite the poor, the crippled, the lame, the blind, and you will be blessed. Although they cannot repay you, you will be repaid at the resurrection of the righteous. (Luke 14:13–14)*

Jesus also cares about children and the elderly—widows specifically. Jesus includes a widow in His parable about persevering prayer (Luke 18:1–8).

Now let's sit for a few minutes at the feet of Jesus as He preaches His Sermon on the Mount. If you heard this for the first time, what would mesmerize you? Open your Bible to Matthew 5, and read and "hear" what Jesus taught both men and women.

📖 Read Matthew 5:3–11

3. Write the "who" for each "blessed."

Poor

Mourning

_____

_____

4. Star the "blessed" you can relate to today and circle which "blessed" you need to be.

5. Skip farther down and read Matthew 5:43–45. What is new and different about Jesus' teaching? "But I tell you…"

_____

_____

Tuck this scripture in the back of your mind. At the time of Jesus' Sermon on the Mount, perhaps no listener could begin to grasp that Jesus would carry out those words as He died on the cross. But Jesus didn't live out His words in noisy proclamations. Skip to the next chapter and read Matthew 6:1–4.

Jesus seems to be encouraging invisible, random acts of kindness. He doesn't applaud the noisy do-gooder, but rather the quiet Christian-in-Action (CIA).

📖 Read on in Matthew 6:25–34.

6. List what Jesus cautions us *not* to worry about (verses 25, 31).

_____

_____

7. What is the ultimate solution to worrying (verse 33)?

_____

_____

> How can _you_ be a CIA today in _quiet_ random acts of kindness?

What reassurance! We women are always planning, considering, and wondering, but Jesus gave a simple solution to those kinds of needless cares: Seek first His kingdom. He goes on to compare His relationship with that of a father and his children. Flip to the next chapter to hear more of His suggestions.

📖 Read Matthew 7:7–11.

8. <u>For what do you need to:</u>   <u>What does the Bible say will happen?</u>

Ask =
Seek =
Knock =

And for all you tired and weary listeners, He encourages us all to come to Him and find rest. This must have been an attractive statement for exhausted women!

The yoke the Master Carpenter can design will be light and specifically tailored for each individual follower. He knows His listeners and He knows their needs.

Jesus' illustrations and stories reassure, encourage, and comfort not just the men; they are also specifically tailored for women. In *Mary Magdalene: Beyond the Myth*, Esther De Boer writes, "He speaks just as easily of the pains of giving birth, leaven, salt, light, water and keeping the house clean, as he does of stewardship, keeping sheep, fishing and being a father."[5]

Today we've listened to the stories of Jesus and His teaching on the mountainside and focused on why it resonated with the women of AD 30. Can you see the simple answers He offered to people weighed down with religiosity? He cared. He loved. He healed. He did then; He longs to do it in your life now.

Jesus' Words in Action: What words of Jesus did you need to hear today? Do you see yourself in any of His stories? What qualities in Jesus draw you near to Him? Since His words are so beautiful and He loves us, how can we share His love and teaching with others? How can *His* story be our story?

> "Come to me, all you who are weary and burdened, and I will give you rest. Take my yoke upon you and learn from me, for I am gentle and humble in heart, and you will find rest for your souls. For my yoke is easy and my burden is light." (Matthew 11:28–30)

Ash Wednesday: How Do We Celebrate the Good News?

I saw my kindergartener's new piano teacher cross the parking lot with an ash mark across her forehead. I didn't want Julia to be scared or ask an inappropriate question, so I bent down and gave Julia a 10-second explanation of what little I knew of Ash Wednesday. Julia's response surprised me: "Can I do that next year, too, Mommy?"

Ash Wednesday is the seventh Wednesday or 46 days prior to Easter and marks the beginning of Lent which focuses on our need for forgiveness and salvation. ' "Forgive us our sins, for we also forgive everyone who sins against us. And lead us not into temptation' " (Luke 11:4).

Some denominations celebrate the Lenten season prior to Easter. Some of the practices and rituals may help participants slow down and focus on Jesus. Those from more highly liturgical churches may be familiar with Stations of the Cross and Ash

Wednesday, but for others these terms may be foreign. Although this is not a liturgical Bible study, biblically based observances can enhance our understanding of Easter and focus our worship.

What Is the Significance of Lent?

Lent originated as *lencten* or "lenthen" of daylight to describe the lengthening of the days. Lent began in the second century as a way of educating new Christians for the forty days prior to their Easter baptism. (What a day to be baptized into the church!)

When we think of Lent, the following words come to mind: penitence, reflection, suffering, death and resurrection, prayer, fasting, discipline, study, contemplation, preparation, introspection, self-examination, repentance, and retreat.

The forty days of Lent begin with Ash Wednesday and end with the Great Vigil of Easter, subtracting all Sundays, which instead celebrate the resurrection. The number *forty* is representative of Jesus' forty days alone in the wilderness to prepare Him for His own spiritual journey.

You, too, can have forty days to prepare for Easter. This may mean turning *away* from certain sinful behaviors and returning *to* God.

Why give up something for Lent? Perhaps it will help you share in His sufferings. Maybe the discipline will help you focus on Him. It may help you experience sorrow over your sin and what it cost the Messiah. It may help you realize that God is ultimately in control, not belongings, desires, or habits.

Experience a new simplicity this season. Get rid of heavy schedules and overtime, and lighten your life. But remember, our *deeds* cannot make God love us any more than He already does. Both giving up something for Lent and adding devotion to our lives help our hearts focus on Him throughout this season.

You've already added something to enhance this Easter season by committing to forty days of study and 16 days of devotionals! As you come closer to Jesus, learn by His example how to respond to the world around you. Be a blessing to others. If you want to add something else for Lent, you could reconcile with a friend, reach out to a neighbor, or read a Lenten devotional.

Even before Christ's resurrection, pagan celebrations and

Jewish feasts were held during the spring. Similarly there was much festivity during December before Christ's birth. However, early Christians set both birth and resurrection dates during secular *holidays* and turned them into *holy* days.

Wearing an ash smudge across the forehead began in the 12th century. Palm branches from the previous year were burned, their ashes mixed with oil, and then a cross was smudged across the Christian's forehead as a constant reminder that we are all sinners and desperately in need of forgiveness. But one pastor at my church, after the mark was placed on each participant's forehead, asked the parishioners to turn to their neighbors and wipe off the mark. The idea was to carry the mark *inwardly*.

Old Testament scriptures showed the remorse and sorrow associated with ashes (Esther 4:1–3; Job 42:6; 2 Samuel 13:19). "O my people, put on sackcloth and roll in ashes; mourn with bitter wailing as for an only son, for suddenly the destroyer will come upon us" (Jeremiah 6:26).

In addition to Ash Wednesday and Lent, there are other terms surrounding the Easter season—some secular, some sacred. If you're like me, you may find these unfamiliar. The definitions below may help you sort out the festivities.

Shrove Tuesday—The Tuesday preceding Ash Wednesday. Shrove means "to repent."

Shrovetide is the three days before Lent (Sunday, Monday, and Tuesday). These same three days are also called "Carnival" meaning "removal of meat," "Mardi Gras," or "Fat Tuesday," a very secular celebration of costumes, parades, dancing and drinking.[6]

Palm Sunday celebrates the day Jesus entered Jerusalem on a donkey to loud shouts of "Hosanna!" Palm Sunday marks the beginning of Holy Week.

Passover commemorates Israel's freedom from Pharoah. Although Egypt's firstborn males were killed during the tenth plague, the Israelites were saved by the mark of the blood of

The Colors of Lent	
Red	Blood of Christ
Black	Sin – Good Friday
Grey	Ashes—Ash Wednesday (sorrow)
Purple	Royalty—King Jesus

Can we ever truly understand His suffering and what He did for us? Probably not. But oh, how we need to grasp our need for a Savior!

the lamb. Similarly, we are saved through the blood of Jesus, the Lamb of God.

Feast of Unleavened Bread is a seven-day Jewish festival following Passover in which no leavening products are used. This festival commemorates the Israelites' hasty flight from Egypt and their arrival to safety.

"The Great Three Days"—*Triduum*

1. Maundy Thursday is the Thursday prior to Easter. Maundy is Latin for *mandatum novum* or "new commandment" remembering Jesus' new commandment recorded in John 13:34. "A new command I give you: Love one another. As I have loved you, so you must love one another." Thursday services remember Jesus' betrayal, the Lord's Supper, His washing the disciples' feet, and His final teachings as recorded in John's Gospel.

2. Good Friday may be an alteration of the term "God's Friday." Good Friday remembers Jesus' crucifixion and His last words from the cross (John 18:1—19:37). On Good Friday a Tenebrae (Latin—*shadows* or *darkness*) service features scriptures, meditations, and extinguished candles as the Christ candle exits the room.[7]

Great Vigil is Holy Saturday or Black Saturday, remembering the dark moments before the resurrection.

3. Easter celebrates Jesus' resurrection from the dead.

Ascension recognizes Jesus' return to heaven, which occurred forty days after Jesus' resurrection.

Pentecost celebrates the gift of the Holy Spirit and is celebrated fifty (pente) days after Passover. It also correlates with the Jewish Festival of the Feast of Weeks, falling seven weeks after the harvest.

The Calendar

Why does Easter move each year? The date is determined by a complicated timetable involving the first full moon and the vernal equinox, making Easter fall sometime between March 22 and April 25. If you're confused about how it's determined, join the centuries of individuals who have tried to find a system for the entire world to celebrate Easter on the same Sunday!

For your *personal* celebration, below are some ideas others have used during Lent. Whatever you choose to do during Lent, be deliberate and intentional, and find a way to experience the forty-day journey the Savior took before Easter.

Celebrate Lent with...

Easter Devotional. Read *Journey to the Cross* by Helen Haidle with your children.

Resurrection Eggs. These eggs for children can be ordered from FamilyLife.com. As an accompaniment, read *Benjamin's Box, A Resurrection Story.*

Lenten Wreath. This is the Advent candle wreath in reverse. Instead of lighting a new candle each of the four Sundays prior to Christmas, on each of the seven Sundays of Lent, you extinguish one of the seven candles until you are left with no candles on Good Friday. Incorporate scripture reading as you extinguish the candles. Re-light all the candles on Easter, for Jesus conquers the darkness![8]

Plan a Walk to observe the signs of spring and creation. Notice the light and joy in the new changes. "For since the creation of the world God's invisible qualities—his eternal power and divine nature—have been clearly seen, being understood from what has been made, so that men are without excuse" (Romans 1:20).

Stations of the Cross. Though begun by early Christians retracing Jesus' steps to Golgotha, both Catholics and Protestants still set apart a time and place to meditate, worship, and give thanks at a series of stations which focus on Christ's journey to the cross.[9]

Memorize one verse each week.

Focus on one of Jesus' seven "I AM" statements each Sunday. To help further pack for our journey, we'll look at two words: "I AM." When Jesus explains He is the **I AM** of the Old Testament, He connects the God of the Old Testament with the Messiah of the New Testament.

The Great I AM

Now we get to peruse an *Old* Testament story with major implications in the *New Testament.* Each time the term I AM is listed throughout this eight-week study, I hope that you will flash back to its Old Testament origins and implications.

In Exodus 3:1–18, we find Moses tending the flock of his father-in-law on Horeb, the mountain of God. The angel of the Lord appears to Him in a flaming bush that is not consumed. God tells Moses to remove his sandals because he is standing on holy ground. "I am the God of your father, the God of Abraham, the God of Isaac and the God of Jacob" (Exodus 3:6).

God then reveals to Moses that He has seen the misery of His people. He's heard their crying, and He wants to rescue them and bring them into a land flowing with milk and honey. He instructs Moses to speak to Pharaoh, but Moses questions God: "Who am I, that I should go to Pharaoh and bring the Israelites out of Egypt?" God reassures Moses He will be with Him. But Moses questions further, "What if they ask your name? Then what should I say?"

God said to Moses, "I AM WHO I AM. This is what you are to say to the Israelites: 'I AM has sent me to you'" (Exodus 3:14). And God further expounds, "This is my name forever, the name by which I am to be remembered from generation to generation" (Exodus 3:15).

> "I AM WHO I AM. This is what you are to say to the Israelites: 'I AM has sent me to you.'" (Exodus 3:14)

I AM is God's name forever. When Jesus says I AM, He's saying He is the God of the past, the God of the present, and the God of the future. He is the God who will save the people from their oppression and persecution and deliver them to a land of milk and honey.

That is why I AM is so profoundly powerful. When Jesus makes the claim, His listeners must choose whether or not to believe Him. "I told you that you would die in your sins; if you do not believe that I am [the one I claim to be], you will indeed die in your sins" (John 8:24). What would *you* think if you heard, "I tell you the truth, before Abraham was born, I am" (John 8:58)? A claim so radical meets with anger. "At this, they picked up stones to stone him, but Jesus hid himself, slipping away from the temple grounds" (John 8:59).

You cannot read the words I AM without understanding both Old and New Testament implications. Today let's look further at the other places where Jesus made I AM claims. After each claim, fill in the blank as to what the accompanying promise means to *you*.

"Then Jesus declared, '**I am** the bread of life. He who comes to me will never go hungry, and he who believes in me will never be thirsty.'" (John 6:35)

"**I am** the living bread that came down from heaven. If anyone eats of this bread, he will live forever. This bread is my flesh, which I will give for the life of the world." (John 6:51)

1. Because Jesus is the Great I AM and the _____ _____ _____, I will _____.

"When Jesus spoke again to the people, he said, '**I am** the light of the world. Whoever follows me will never walk in darkness, but will have the light of life.'" (John 8:12)

2. Because Jesus is the great I AM and the _____ ___ ___ _____, I will _____.

"Therefore Jesus said again, 'I tell you the truth, **I am** the gate for the sheep." (John 10:7)

"**I am** the gate; whoever enters through me will be saved. He will come in and go out, and find pasture." (John 10:9)

3. Because Jesus is the great I AM and the _____ ____ _____ _____, I can enter and _____.

"**I am** the good shepherd. The good shepherd lays down his life for the sheep." (John 10:11)

"I am the good shepherd; I know my sheep and my sheep know me— just as the Father knows me and I know the Father—and I lay down my life for the sheep." (John 10:14–15)

4. Because Jesus is the great I AM and the _____ _____, He will _____ and I will _____.

"Jesus said to her, '**I am** the resurrection and the life. He who believes in me will live, even though he dies.'" (John 11:25)

5. Because Jesus is the great I AM and the _____ ____ _____ _____, I will _____.

"Jesus answered, '**I am** the way and the truth and the life. No one comes to the Father except through me.'" (John 14:6)

6. Because Jesus is the Great I AM and the _____ and the _____ and the _____, I can _____.

"**I am** the true vine, and my Father is the gardener." (John 15:1)

> I AM the
> Bread of Life
> Light of the World
> Gate (Door) for the Sheep
> Good Shepherd
> Resurrection and the Life
> Way, Truth, Life
> True Vine

"**I am** the vine; you are the branches. If a man remains in me and I in him, he will bear much fruit; apart from me you can do nothing." (John 15:5)

7. Because Jesus is the great I AM and the _____ _____, through Him I will _____.

In Revelation, we will see that HE is also the Alpha and Omega, the beginning and the end, the Root and Offspring of David, and the bright Morning Star.

"**I am** the Alpha and the Omega, the First and the Last, the Beginning and the End." (Revelation 22:13)

"I, Jesus, have sent my angel to give you this testimony for the churches. **I am** the Root and the Offspring of David, and the bright Morning Star." (Revelation 22:16)

Jesus' Words in Action: Most of the time when I'm having problems, it's because *I am* focusing on *myself*. My sentences begin with *I am* instead of claiming promises and proclaiming the power of the *great* I Am.

Lent encourages us to focus on Jesus. In obedience to His teaching, how can you "fast" from doing something that causes sin or add a loving action? In what ways can your spiritual journey be enhanced by the discipline of constantly remembering what He did for you? Do you know that by looking *back* at the death you deserved to die, you can look *forward* to the life you will have in Him?

Walter Wangerin explains,

> …when we genuinely remember the death we deserve to die, we will be moved to remember the death the Lord in fact did die—because his took the place of ours. Ah, children, we will yearn to hear the Gospel story again and again, ever seeing therein our death in his, and rejoicing that we will therefore know a rising like his as well.[10]

Thursday: Why Did They Want a King? Why Did They Need a Savior?

What are you waiting for? The Jews of Matthew, Mark, Luke, and John were waiting for religious and political freedom. Their wait had been long. Your Bible, with its sliver-thin pages, reveals no gap between the Old and the New Testaments.

However, there are four hundred years of waiting. There was little to write, because the people weren't listening and God wasn't speaking through the prophets. God broke a long silence by finally letting Zechariah know that his son, John, would prepare the way for the Messiah. And when the Word (Jesus Christ) was made flesh, the Word began fulfilling the Old Testament prophecy about Jesus.

What was happening in the region to magnify their longing for release?

Let's look at a map of Palestine. On the map on the following page, you'll see Israel is divided into regions, including Judea, Samaria, Galilee, Phoenicia, and Idumea. On the East side of the Jordan River you'll see Decapolis and Perea. Note the familiar cities of Capernaum, Emmaus, Nazareth, Caesarea, Jerusalem, Bethany, and points of interest such as the Sea of Galilee, River Jordan, Mount of Olives (Olivet), and the Dead Sea. Let's focus primarily on Judea, Samaria, and Galilee.

You'll note that Rome is not on the map; it's too far away. And yet Rome is the long-distance governing power. This creates political problems and control issues. Rome is added to the long series of oppressive governments.

During the Intertestamental Period, the Jews were under the thumbs of four successive empires:

Assyrian, (750–612 BC), Babylonian (612–539 BC), Persian (539–331 BC), and Greek (331–146 BC). The Maccabees at last gave the Jews a short independence. However, Roman occupation followed in 63 BC and on into the first century with Herod the Great ruling the Jews. Is it any wonder the Jews wanted their independence and freedom?

Politically

Rome appointed certain rulers to represent the Jews. King Herod the Great ruled at the time of Jesus' birth. When Herod died, he divided his region among his sons, none of whom respected the Jews. Questioning the rulers resulted in death. Herod's son, Herod Antipas, ruled during Jesus' time in Jerusalem. He was more interested in political power than Jewish faith. Herod Antipas had to keep peace at all costs.

Palestine in the Time of Jesus

- Extent of Herod's kingdom
- Herodian fortress city
- Decapolis city (time of Herod)
- Other city
- Mountain

Spiritually

Chief Priests/Sadducees tended to be worldly and tempted to compromise in order to position themselves well with the Romans. John the Baptist warned the Pharisees and Sadducees to produce fruit in keeping with repentance (Matthew 3:8) and that "The ax is already at the root of the trees, and every tree that does not produce good fruit will be cut down and thrown into the fire" (Matthew 3:10). But the religious leaders did not want someone marching into Jerusalem and causing such a disturbance that they would lose what little power they had.

Though the Jews wanted a powerful political leader who would represent them, they really needed a spiritual king: Jesus of Nazareth. Let's look at Jesus at the point when He announces He is the One prophesied in the Old Testament.

Luke 4 opens with Jesus being led by the Spirit in the desert for forty days of fasting. Jesus refutes the devil's temptations of food and power by quoting Scriptures. After forty days, Jesus returns to Galilee where His fame has spread. But it is his return to *Nazareth* that prompts the familiar quote, "A prophet is not recognized in his own country" (John 4:44, Mark 6:4, Luke 4:24).

📖 Read Luke 4:16–30.

As a Jewish Rabbi, Jesus taught in all the Galilean synagogues. Jesus' listeners sat in rows of benches in the synagogue, in what amounted to a community center. Wouldn't you love to have sat at Jesus' feet and heard Him read from God's Word? Wouldn't it have been wonderful to hear Him explain the truths of His Father?[11]

At synagogue, a chosen leader goes to the Moses seat and reads from a pre-selected passage of scripture from the Torah: the five books of Moses, God's covenant with Israel. On that *particular* Sabbath day, in Jesus' hometown, God made Jesus the synagogue reader and gave Him the scriptures for the day, which would announce who He was. No coincidence—a God-incidence![12]

1. What is given to Jesus on the Sabbath in the synagogue (verse 17)?

_____

The *Word made flesh* holds the *Word of God*. Jesus unrolls the scripture and reads from Isaiah 61:1 and part of verse 2, stopping short of the passage on judgment.

2. Because the Spirit of the Lord is upon Him, what does this passage tell us Jesus has the power to do (verses 18–19)?

_____

Jesus returns the scroll and sits down. The eyes of everyone in the synagogue are fastened on Jesus (Luke 4:20). Wouldn't you have loved to be there for that scene? There must have been a hushed moment of anticipation.

And then He completes the teaching by adding the crux of the message, *"Today this scripture is fulfilled in your hearing"* (Luke 4:21). So far He has merely read the Word. Now He reveals that He *is* the Word.

3. What are some of their initial reactions (verse 22)?

_____

4. What other proverb does Jesus quote in response (verse 23)?

_____

> "The Spirit of the Sovereign LORD is on me, because the LORD has anointed me to preach good news to the poor. He has sent me to bind up the brokenhearted, to proclaim freedom for the captives and release from darkness for the prisoners, to proclaim the year of the LORD's favor…"

5. What does Jesus claim they will ask of Him (verse 23)?

_____

Jesus then recalls Old Testament incidents where healing came to *one* instead of *many*. This incites Jesus' listeners to drive Him out of town and attempt to throw Him off the cliff. What a terrible way to end synagogue for the day!

6. Why did Jesus' words infuriate them?

_____

_____

Luke 4:30 says that Jesus walks right through the crowd and continues on His way. Jesus will do that. He knows His time, His mission, and His purpose. He knows that in Nazareth, the people lack faith and so He will not exercise His power in Nazareth as He did in Capernaum.

Jesus' purpose was determined before the beginning of time, before the creation of the world, and before man ever sinned. In other words, God planned salvation before there was time. Read the scriptures below to note how early our grace was promised.

"This grace was given us in Christ Jesus *before the beginning of time.*" (2 Timothy 1:9)

"He was chosen before the creation of the world, but was revealed in these last times for your sake." (1 Peter 1:20)

". . . a faith and knowledge resting on the hope of eternal life, which God, who does not lie, promised before the beginning of time." (Titus 1:2)

In the Old Testament, there had to be atonement for sins through the lifeblood of a sacrifice. The Old Testament said that "the life of a creature is in the blood, and I have given it to you to make atonement for yourselves on the altar; it is the blood that makes atonement for one's life" (Leviticus 17:11). The New Testament confirms that, "In fact, the law requires that nearly everything be cleansed with blood, and without the shedding of blood there is no forgiveness" (Hebrews 9:22).

📖 Read what Jesus has done in Hebrews 9:11–14.

7. What does the blood of goats accomplish (verse 13)?

_____

_____

8. What is the greater and more perfect tabernacle?

_____

_____

9. How are we now inwardly clean (verse 14)?

_____

_____

10. What does the blood of Christ accomplish (verse 14)?

_____

_____

The *old* has been done away, and Jesus is the *new* sacrifice, as well as the perfect Priest. The Messiah came to take away our sins, to bind and heal our wounds, and make us inwardly clean so that we may serve Him with a clear conscience. That's the kind of King we all need.

Jesus' Words in Action: In John 10:10, Jesus revealed that He came to bring life to the fullest. But this wasn't what the Jews were seeking. What about you? What do you need from Jesus? Do you want the life and the fullness of life Jesus offers? Read again Christ's revelation from Isaiah 61. Have you really listened to His Good News? Are you ready to let Him bind your broken heart and be free?

Friday: What Was It Like to Be a Woman in AD 30?

Women's lives have changed significantly over the last 2000 years. To understand how Jesus appeared to the women of his time and to know why Jesus seemed so radical and liberating, we have to return to the first century. Put down your pen, you won't need it today. Enjoy reading. This information will allow you to travel back in time and see Jesus anew.

Clothing

As a woman you wear a linen petticoat (*kolbu*) as well as a dress (Baldinajja linene). A robe is tied over this (*Istomukhvia*) and a scarf wrapped around your waist (*Pirzomata*). You also wear a girdle the colors of your tribe's stripes. A scarf hides your face.[13]

Social Interactions

As you move about, you are not to talk to men. The Jewish writings of the *Talmud* and *Mishna,* as well as the religious leaders discourage men from speaking to women because it might be misinterpreted or lead to adultery.[14]

Philip Yancey writes,

> In social life, few women would talk to men outside of their families, and a woman was to touch no man but her spouse. Yet Jesus associated freely with women and taught some as his disciples. A Samaritan woman who had been through five husbands, Jesus tapped to lead a spiritual revival (notably, he began the conversation by asking **her** for help). A prostitute's anointing, he accepted with gratitude. Women traveled with his band of followers, no doubt stirring up much gossip. Women populated Jesus' parables and illustrations, and frequently he did miracles on their behalf.[15]

In other words, Jesus violates the rules, treating women as equals, something unheard of during that time.[16]

Education

If you feel shunned socially, it continues into the classroom. Your education includes religion, reading, and writing, but usually stops when you achieve a minimum. A boy or man's education continues longer than a girl's.[17]

Religious Education and Practice

You have had limited religious teaching and practice. The Torah is for men; the spindle for women.[18] It is a patriarchal society where men hold the power in politics as well as religion.

The religious "Supreme Court" or Sanhedrin is a men-only club. They alone can wear scriptures on their foreheads. The temple was also a men-only club except for the women's court. Women *can* worship by doing good works. The women *can* prepare for the Sabbath by cooking three kosher meals, filling lamps, filling jugs with water, cleaning the house, washing laundry.[20] But there is plenty they *cannot* do.

Number of Times Men and Women are Mentioned in the Gospels	
Daughters—24	Sons—327
Mothers—72	Fathers—293
Woman/women—78	Man/men—295 [19]

Women were not permitted to pray, in public or at home. In the synagogue they were set apart from the men, hidden behind a screen. They couldn't bear legal witness, nor did their presence in the assembly count toward a quorum. Not to mention the fact that rabbis did not speak to women in public.[21]

Jesus changed this. Yancey writes, "To take just one example of the revolutionary changes Jesus set in motion, consider Jesus' attitude toward women. In those days, at every synagogue service Jewish men pray, 'Blessed art thou, O Lord, who hast not made me a woman.'"[22]

But when Mary sits listening at Jesus' feet, there is no rebuke. Jesus applauds her and says she has chosen the good part. Jesus actually encourages women to follow, listen, and grow spiritually.[23]

Laws of Purity

For men, not only is it "Don't talk to a woman in public" but also "Don't touch." If you as a woman are considered unclean, you can make others unclean. What makes you unclean? Menstruation is one thing. Your impurity lasts seven days and anything you sit on or lay down on is considered unclean. Anyone touching your bed or anything you sit on has to wash his or her clothes and take a bath. A man who has relations with you will be considered unclean for seven more days, and his bed is considered unclean, too! (Leviticus 15:19–24).

Rabbis encourage safety and so they have added days before and after the seven, warning of the possibility of death from contamination.[24]

Childbirth also makes you ceremonially unclean for seven days following the birth. You aren't purified for another thirty-three days after that. You can't go into the sanctuary or touch anything sacred until that time is over. That's if you have a boy. But if you give birth to a girl, the period of uncleanness was *twice* the length (Leviticus 12:1–8).

But Jesus touched women, and when a bleeding and thus "unclean" woman touched *Him*, He recognized her faith and did not rebuke her (Mark 5:25–34).[25]

What is different about Jesus? He is more interested in the women's faith. He is more concerned about what is on the *inside* than the *outside*, the spiritual rather than the physical.[26] Jesus knows that what comes from a person's *heart* is what makes him unclean. Evil comes from the inside out (Mark 7:21–23).

Yancey describes how sickeningly radical Jesus appeared to the Pharisees. He was out to change the system and liberate the unclean.

> In the midst of this religious caste system, Jesus appeared. To the Pharisees' dismay he had no qualms about socializing with children or sinners or even Samaritans. He touched, or was touched by, the "unclean": those with leprosy, the deformed, a hemorrhaging woman, the lunatic and possessed. Although Levitical laws prescribed a day of purification after touching a sick person, Jesus conducted mass healings in which he touched scores of sick people; he never concerned himself with the rules of defilement after contact with the sick or even the dead.[27]

Legal

Legally, women have fewer rights, decisions, and little power. You can't own land, and you are not a valid witness in court. A widow cannot inherit; the money stays in her husband's family and she is at their mercy for her care. If you are unmarried when your parents die, the inheritance goes to your brother.

When Jesus arrives, He is concerned for the widows. His half-brother went on to write, "Religion that God our Father accepts as pure and faultless is this: to look after orphans and widows in their distress and to keep oneself from being polluted by the world" (James 1:27).

In Old Testament writings, females did not hold the same financial value as males. A male (age 20–60) dedicated to the Lord was worth fifty shekels of silver whereas a female was worth thirty (Leviticus 27:1–5). Children were worth less than that. But followers of Jesus went on to write, "There is neither Jew nor Greek, slave nor free, male nor female, for you are all one in Christ Jesus" (Galatians 3:28).

Jesus values the women and children even though Gospel writers don't count them in the feeding of the thousands and turned the children away (Matthew 14:21, 15:38; Mark 10:14–15).[28] Similarly, Jesus does not show partiality in His treatment. Jesus heals and teaches both men and women. "Jesus' actions, when contrasted with the dictums of the rabbis, makes it clear that Christ's coming introduces a redemptive process designed to lift and restore women to the position they enjoyed in original creation." [29]

The Family

While motherhood is considered beautiful, being in the family of God is what Jesus emphasizes. He explains that the blessedness was not in the suckling of a child but in being comforted by God, in hearing God's Word and obeying it (Luke 11:27–28).[30]

> *"As Jesus was saying these things, a woman in the crowd called out, 'Blessed is the mother who gave you birth and nursed you.' He replied, "Blessed rather are those who hear the word of God and obey it" (Luke 11:27–28).*

With Jesus, once again, the status of the heart is more important than family structure and marital status. Similarly, he reveals that His family members are those who do His Father's will. He begins bringing equality to family roles.[31]

Marriage and Divorce

Married women have few marital rights and are vulnerable to divorce for invalid reasons, depending

> "'Who are my mother and my brothers?' he asked. Then he looked at those seated in a circle around him and said, 'Here are my mother and my brothers!' " (Mark 3:34–35)

on who is interpreting the law. It is less probable that a woman could start divorce proceedings. In AD 30, a husband can just say, "You are divorced," but at least the Jews require a certificate to obtain a legal divorce.[32]

Jesus reminds listeners that divorce is also an issue of the heart, a hard one, and not a part of God's created plan. God created male and female to unite and become one flesh. "Therefore what God has joined together, let man not separate" (Mark 10:5–9).

He warns that getting a divorce is more than just handing out a certificate and notes that *both* parties have equal responsibility in the marriage.[33]

> "He answered, 'Anyone who divorces his wife and marries another woman commits adultery against her. And if she divorces her husband and marries another man, she commits adultery.' "
> (Mark 10:11–12)

Country/City

The rules are stricter for a woman of Jerusalem than for a woman in the country. The wealthy Sadducees exert a great deal of control over the temple and own a significant amount of money; whereas the priests in more rural areas are as poor as the fishermen, artisans, shopkeepers, and farmers they serve. The wives also might have worked to sell their husband's produce.

Author Sue Richards sums up today's lesson well,

> Women, who ever since the Fall had taken a lowly place in human society and even in Israel's faith, are lifted up and given striking prominence by Jesus Christ. Christ consistently displayed a concern for women that contrasts sharply with the way women were viewed and treated in first-century Jewish society.[34]

As you can see, Jesus changes women's lives for the better. From Christ's genealogy to His birth and then to His interaction with others, women take on important roles. Jesus' genealogy includes five women: Rahab (prostitute), Tamar (had sex with father-in-law), Ruth (Moabitess), the wife of Uriah (had adulterous relationship with King David), and Mary the mother of Jesus (poor young peasant girl).

God sent His only Son to be born of a *female*. "But when the time had fully come, God sent his Son, born of a woman, born under law" (Galatians 4:4). God transformed the lives of those in the genealogy as well as—through His Son—the lives of all women.

Though it might appear that women are in the *background* in the first century, it's just that the lights haven't been turned up on their part of the stage. Though I'm not a feminist, I am moved by how Jesus cares for women, and I delight in flooding the stage to highlight Jesus' transformative power in our lives.

Jot down any information you can remember about the women listed below next to their names. If there are lots of blanks, good! Then the study for the next two weeks will seem new and fresh!

New Testament Women Jesus encountered—You'll meet them in the next two weeks:

Jairus' daughter and wife

Hemorrhaging woman (How would you like to be remembered for *that*?)

Syrophoenecian woman

Mary Magdalene

Peter's mother-in-law

Woman at the well

Mary/Martha

Adulterous woman (A name worse than *hemorrhaging!*)

Bent, crippled woman

Widow at Nain

Anointing woman

Salome

Jesus' Words in Action: As Jesus interacted with women, He affirmed their value, challenged their faith, and broke society's rules.[35] What about you? Can you see that Jesus wants you to sit at His feet and listen to His teaching? How has Jesus changed your life, and how can He further transform you? It's exciting to know what a relationship with your Savior can offer!

Saturday: "Near the Cross"

By Fanny Crosby

Scripture: "Near the cross of Jesus stood his mother, his mother's sister, Mary the wife of Clopas, and Mary Magdalene." (John 19:25)

What drew the women to the cross? In this beloved hymn,

> "*Near the cross! O Lamb of God, bring its scenes before me; Help me walk from day to day, with its shadows over me.*"
>
> *"Near the Cross" by Fanny Crosby*

composer Fanny Crosby asked Jesus to keep her near the cross. Would it surprise you to know that she was blind? And yet her hymn celebrates a precious fountain, morning star, a healing stream flowing from Calvary. She recognizes the privilege of being tucked in the shadow of the cross. How poignant her request to "bring its scenes before me!" Indeed, may we, too, really see the cross this Lenten season.

"Near the Cross"

Jesus, keep me near the cross, there a precious fountain
Free to all, a healing stream flows from Calvary's mountain.

Refrain:
In the cross, in the cross, be my glory ever;
Till my raptured soul shall find— rest beyond the river.

Near the cross, a trembling soul, love and mercy found me;
There the bright and morning star sheds its beams around me.

Refrain:
Near the cross! O Lamb of God, bring its scenes before me;
Help me walk from day to day, with its shadows over me.

Response: *Lord Jesus, Keep me near the cross today and always. May I glory only in the cross. O Lamb of God, in my own spiritual blindness, help me see the scenes from the cross and be transformed by them.*

Sunday: "Hallelujah! What a Savior!"

By Philip Bliss

Scripture: "Look, the Lamb of God, who takes away the sin of the world!" (John 1:29b)

For liturgical churches that observe Lent, Sunday is a day off. It's a day off from fasting and work to celebrate the resurrection. What better way to celebrate than to repeat after each description of Christ "Hallelujah! What a Savior!"

The song lacks any formal verse/chorus format, but this *Easter* hymn, like most *Christmas* carols, ends focusing on Jesus' second coming. We cannot celebrate Christmas without Easter, and we cannot fully celebrate Christmas or Easter without the knowledge that one day Jesus will return! We will see Him face to face and be able to sing, "Hallelujah! What a Savior!"

"Hallelujah! What a Savior!"

"Man of Sorrows!" what a name for the Son of God,
Who came ruined sinners to reclaim! Hallelujah, what a Savior!

Bearing shame and scoffing rude, in my place condemned He
*   stood*
Sealed my pardon with His blood: Hallelujah, what a Savior!

*Guilty, vile and helpless we, spotless **Lamb of God** was He;*
Full atonement! Can it be? Hallelujah, what a Savior!

Lifted up was He to die, "It is finished," was His cry;
Now in heav'n exalted high: Hallelujah, what a Savior!

When He comes, our glorious King, all His ransomed home to
*   bring,*
Then anew this song we'll sing: Hallelujah! What a Savior!

One day, Jesus will come again and this second coming will be met with loud Hallelujahs. Maybe that's why the Hallelujahs in the Bible are found in Revelation—a book about His *second* coming!

Response: Lord Jesus, thank you for enduring the cross for me. I am slowly learning what shame, condemnation, and sorrow you felt. But now you are exalted high and Your Name is above all names. "Hallelujah, what a Savior!" I long for the day of your return when I will worship You face to face.

> "After this I heard what sounded like the roar of a great multitude in heaven shouting: "Hallelujah! Salvation and glory and power belong to our God" (Revelation 19:1).

Works Cited

1. Maier, Paul L., *In the Fullness of Time: A Historian Looks at Christmas, Easter, and the Early Church* (Grand Rapids, MI: Kregel, 1991), 182.

2. Ibid., 91.

3. Ibid., 91, 93.

4. Yancey, Philip, *The Jesus I Never Knew* (Grand Rapids, MI: Zondervan, 1995), 88.

5. De Boer, Esther, *Mary Magdalene: Beyond the Myth* (Harrisburg, PA: Trinity Press International, 1996), 36–37.

6. Dennis Bratcher, "The Season of Lent," http://www.cresourcei.org.

7. Bratcher, "The Days of Holy Week," http://www.cresourcei.org.

8. Noel Piper, "The Light Shines in Darkness," Proverbs 31 Woman, March 2005.

9. Bratcher, "The Cross as a Journey," http://www.cresourcei.org.

10. Wangerin, Walter Jr., *Reliving the Passion: Meditations on the Suffering Death and Resurrection of Jesus as Recorded in Mark* (Grand Rapids, MI: Zondervan, 1992), 22.

11. Ray Vander Laan and Focus on the Family Video (That the World May Know Series), *Faith Lessons on the Life and Ministry of the Messiah: The Rabbi* (Grand Rapids, MI: Zondervan, 1996, 1998), Volume 3, Video 2.

12. Ibid.,

13. Bishop, Jim, *The Day Christ Died: The Inspiring Classic on the Last 24 Hours of Jesus' Life* (San Francisco: Harper, 1957), 51.

14. Richards, Sue and Larry, *Every Woman in the Bible* (Nashville, TN: Thomas Nelson, 1999), 153.

15. Yancey, 153–154.

16. Richards, 153.

17. Bishop, 50.

18. Richards, 158–159.

19. Ibid.,

20. Weaver, Joanna, *Having a Mary Heart in a Martha World: Finding Intimacy with God in the Busyness of Life* (Colorado Springs, CO: WaterBrook Press, 2000), 52.

21. Higgs, Liz Curtis, *Mad Mary: A Bad Girl from Magdala, Transformed at His Appearing* (Colorado Springs, CO: WaterBrook Press, 2001), 184.

22. Yancey, 153.

23. Richards, 159.

24. Ibid.,

25. De Boer, Esther, *Mary Magdalene: Beyond the Myth* (Harrisburg, PA: Trinity Press International, 1996), 36.

26. Ibid., 32.

27. Yancey, 153.

28. De Boer, 36.

29. Richards, 155.

30. De Boer, 33.

31. Ibid., 34.

32. Gower, Ralph, *The New Manners and Customs of Bible Times* (Chicago: Moody Press, 1987), 70.

33. De Boer, 33.

34. Richards, 166.

35. Ibid., 160.

WEEK TWO:

TRAVELING WITH JESUS

Five Women Touched by Him

Monday: Jesus Heals Peter's Mother-in-Law

Our bags are packed with background material to help us get to know the many women we'll meet in the next two weeks. First we'll meet Simon Peter's mother-in-law. By the way, Peter is a recurring character in our study. Though Jesus lauds Peter's faith as the type of faith upon which He would build His church, Peter still has much to learn (Matthew 16:18).

The setting is the Sabbath day, and we'll witness Jesus' miraculous healing power. Look back at your map from Week One (page 16). Peter's mother-in-law lives in Capernaum, a city on the Sea of Galilee and the hometown of Peter, Andrew, James, and John. This city buzzes with activity because it's on the caravan route to Damascus and is a customs station and Roman garrison.

Note Capernaum is only twenty-five miles northeast of Nazareth, where Jesus has just revealed His purpose to a disbelieving hometown audience. But after Jesus leaves Nazareth, He puts His *words in action*, touching the life of Peter's family.

📖 Read Luke 4:38–39; Mark 1:29–34 (also Matthew 8:14–15).

(Sometimes you will note passages in parenthesis next to requested reading. These are parallel passages only for those who desire additional research.) Place a bookmark at Luke 4 and Mark 1.

1. Who asks Jesus to help Peter's mother-in-law (Mark 1:29–30)?

_____

2. Who witnesses the miracle (Mark 1:29–30)?

_____

3. Jesus rebukes demons; what else does He rebuke (Luke 4:39)?

_____

Sometimes Jesus heals "long-distance," and sometimes He heals in an "up close and personal" fashion. Matthew 8:15 says that He touched Peter's mother-in-law's hand. I find myself jealous. How comforting to slip one's hand in the Savior's and find healing!

4. How soon is Peter's mother-in-law healed (Mark 1:31; Luke 4:39)?

_____

Her recovery time is amazing. When I recover from a fever, it's a gradual return to normalcy. A slow tingle overcomes my body as my energy is restored. Gradually I can eat food and begin to tackle the housework. I don't look my best after sweating for days, so if the "whole town" gathered at my door after my near-death experience, I wouldn't be *thrilled to death* to entertain (Mark 1:33)!

5. Yet, through the power of Jesus, what does this woman do (Luke 4:39)?

_____

The King James Version says, "immediately she arose and ministered unto them." What a beautiful description of thankful service.

6. What should we be doing as Jesus is at work in our lives (Mark 1:31)?

_____

_____

7. How do you think Peter's mother-in-law felt about the work of her son-in-law after she was healed?

_____

8. How do Jesus' actions fulfill prophecy from Isaiah 53:4?

_____

"Surely he took up our infirmities and carried our sorrows, yet we considered him stricken by God, smitten by him, and afflicted."
(Isaiah 53:4)

9. If you were one of the many men and women outside the door, what do you think your thoughts about this Healer and Teacher would be?

_____

10. Even before the sun sets, what follows this very personal healing (Luke 4: 40)?

_____

_____

Mark adds more details about the character of Jesus. After the whole town has gathered at Peter's mother-in-law's door and Jesus has healed diseases and driven out demons, Mark adds, "Very early in the morning, while it was still dark, Jesus got up, left the house and went off to a solitary place, where he prayed" (Mark 1:35).

Once Jesus' followers catch up and let Him know everyone is looking for Him, Jesus responds, "Let us go somewhere else—to the nearby villages—so I can preach there also. That is why I have come" (Mark 1:38). Jesus knew His mission. Yes, He came to heal, but He has a message to preach. And in order to successfully prepare for His mission, He needs time alone with the Father.

Jesus' Words in Action: Does your day begin in prayer? Do you jumpstart your morning by spending time with the Father? Do you know your mission for the day? What better way to begin a day than to imitate Jesus' priorities. Even if you can't pray or study for hours during this Lenten season, try to spend the first waking moments giving praise and thanksgiving to God. Then lay your day's requests before Him. Put your hand in Jesus' hand; let Him touch you today. Close by meditating on the following verses where the psalmist calls out, "in the morning!"

"*In the morning*, O LORD, you hear my voice; *in the morning* I lay my requests before you and wait in expectation." (Psalm 5:3)

"But I will sing of your strength, *in the morning* I will sing of your love; for you are my fortress, my refuge in times of trouble." (Psalm 59:16)

"But I cry to you for help, O LORD; *in the morning* my prayer comes before you." (Psalm 88:13)

"Satisfy us *in the morning* with your unfailing love, that we may sing for joy and be glad all our days." (Psalm 90:14)

Tuesday: No Accidental Encounter with the Woman at the Well

Have you ever felt you just don't belong? Or perhaps you wonder if your background is too complicated to fit into any Christian setting. Look at Jesus' genealogy and you'll see He was descended from a line of imperfect individuals. Jesus came to earth and reached out to the poor, sick, sinners, and, in today's example, someone who doesn't even reach out to Him. Today we'll meet the Samaritan woman at the well.

Refresh your memory and recall the story of the Good Samaritan. To the Jews, the term "Good Samaritan" would have been oxymoronic. "Good" and "Samaritan" could hardly co-exist in the same sentence. But just why were Samaritans hated?

Their feud dates back more than seven hundred years before Jesus was born, when Jews and Assyrians intermarried. The Assyrians deported thirty thousand Israelites out of the region of Samaria, which was then resettled with foreigners. Though these resettlers believed in Yahweh, they mixed in their own beliefs (2 Kings 17:3–24). Pure Jews hated these new converts and the defilement of their race and religion.[1] Though Samaritans observed the Pentateuch, they were excluded from Jerusalem's temple. They were so despised that Jewish travelers would go *around* Samaria rather than *through* it. Pharisees considered contact with Samaritans contaminating.[2]

But Jesus doesn't believe in *going around* Samaria or going down the *other side* of the street to avoid someone. He makes that very clear when an expert of the law asks Him, "*Who is my neighbor?*" and Jesus tells the following story of "The Good Samaritan."

As the story goes, robbers attack a traveler and leave him stripped and beaten on the road. A priest and Levite pass him by on the *other side* of the road. But the Samaritan takes pity on the man, dresses his wounds, brings him to an inn, and pays for his recovery. The merciful Samaritan is considered the *neighbor*, in contrast to the religious leaders, who walk past the injured man (Luke 10:27–37).

In another scenario, Jesus heals ten lepers (Luke 17:11–19). The *only* one who returns to thank and praise Him is the foreigner, or Samaritan.

Jesus' stories and His actions reveal He is breaking down walls of prejudice and hatred. Jesus has come for all. The Samaritan woman at the well could have been a woman to avoid. But Jesus, who dines with tax collectors and sinners, doesn't operate that way.

> "He threw himself at Jesus' feet and thanked him—and he was a Samaritan." (Luke 17:16)

Our reading today is simplified by the fact that John is the only Gospel writer who records this encounter. It follows John's account of Nicodemus' questions about how to be born again and Jesus' response with the familiar verse: John 3:16.

Before we journey on to the well, tuck these verses about salvation in the back of your mind.

> *This is the verdict: Light has come into the world, but men loved darkness instead of light because their deeds were evil. Everyone who does evil hates the light, and will not come into the light for fear that his deeds will be exposed. But whoever lives by the truth comes into the light, so that it may be seen plainly that what he has done has been done through God. (John 3:19–21)*

The Samaritan woman comes out of the darkness and steps into the light of Christ's love. Read her story as a beautiful story of love and redemption. Don't stop to ask questions; just read the account, and then we'll analyze it together.

> "For God so loved the world that he gave his one and only Son, that whoever believes in him shall not perish but have eternal life." (John 3:16)

Read John 4:4–42

The Samaritan woman probably feels ostracized from her community. Rather than coming to the well in the cool morning hours when other women would enjoy socializing, she arrives during the sixth hour, which could be noon (Jewish time) or more likely six o'clock in the evening (Roman time).[3] At this hour she expects to be alone.

Earlier, Jesus had left Judea and journeyed twenty miles in the heat and dust back to Galilee,[4] and He deliberately did not go down the *other side* of the road. Instead of avoiding Samaria, He went straight through it to the heart of the village of Sychar to meet someone whose life He planned to change.

Their conversation would make a great radio drama because it's almost completely dialogue. But it might be more easily translated on film where subtitles could run beneath to explain the language barrier. The Samaritan woman is talking about H_2O, and He is talking about the *living water* of salvation.

1. Who initiates the discussion? In light of what you know about the relationship between men and women, why is this unusual (verse 7)?

_____

_____

2. What surprises the woman about Jesus' request (verse 9)?

_____

_____

Because she is a Samaritan, a Jew would not have shared utensils with her.[5] But Jesus' dialogue continues on another level. He has asked for H_2O from a deep well, but it is the woman herself who needs living water.

3. What is the "*gift of God*" (verse 10)?

_____

> "If you knew the gift of God and who it is that asks you for a drink, you would have asked him and he would have given you living water." (John 4:10)

Living water flows; it is pure and drinkable as opposed to dead water in cisterns made by man. To enter the synagogue, a Jew would wash in *living water* to be purified. When we're dry and thirsty, it is only the Living Water of Jesus that can cleanse and fulfill us.[6]

4. Read the following scriptures and underline what you learn about living water from them.

"'Whoever believes in me, as the Scripture has said, streams of living water will flow from within him.' By this he meant the Spirit, whom those who believed in him were later to receive." (John 7:38–39a)

"For the Lamb at the center of the throne will be their shepherd; he will lead them to springs of living water. And God will wipe away every tear from their eyes." (Revelation 7:17)

"O LORD, the hope of Israel, all who forsake you will be put to shame. Those who turn away from you will be written in the dust because they have forsaken the LORD, the spring of living water." (Jeremiah 17:13)

5. Jesus' response to the woman's question in John 4:12 is listed below. Fill in the blanks from John 4:13–14.

"_____ who drinks this water will be thirsty again, but whoever drinks the water I give him will _____ thirst. Indeed, the water I give him will become in him a _____ of water welling up to_____ _____." (John 4:13–14)

The words *everyone* and *never* are strong. She wants *living water* and she's open to change. That's when Jesus shifts gears and suddenly tells her to call her husband and return. When she responds that she doesn't have a husband, she is being truthful to a degree. She's had *five* husbands, and the man she's with currently is *not* her husband. Jesus knows more than any stranger *should* know about her. With that kind of knowledge He has to be a prophet! She then talks about one of the differences in the Samaritan and Jewish faiths—where God is worshiped.

But Jesus explains, *where* He is worshipped is not the point. Differences in ethnicity would no longer divide. Jesus explains, we need to worship in spirit and in truth. What does *spirit and truth* mean? Are we *true* worshippers, or are we stuck in subtleties that divide believers? Are we the kind of worshippers the Father seeks?

The Samaritan woman then remarks that the Messiah will come. Jesus' answers, "I who speak to you am he." Right here Jesus claims to be the great "I AM" from Exodus 3:14, which we studied in Week One.

And while we eagerly await the woman's response, the disciples interrupt, surprised to find Jesus talking with a *woman*. Curiously, the Gospel writer John does not report anyone asking, "What do you want?" or "Why are you talking with her?" but instead, records that the reaction of the woman is to leave her water jar behind and return to town. Consider for a moment that it is *after* the conversation that the disciples return. Who might have been the silent observer and recorder of the previous, seemingly private conversation?[7]

The woman who wouldn't draw water with a crowd races into town proclaiming, "Come, see a man who told me everything I ever did. Could this be the Christ?" (John 4:29). Her encounter with Jesus has transformed her. This has been a

> "Yet a time is coming and has now come when the true worshipers will worship the Father in spirit and truth, for they are the kind of worshipers the Father seeks." (John 4:23)

great counseling session. Someone knew her story and background and loved her anyway!

The woman's testimony resonates, and because of her witness, many believe. At the urging of the Samaritan people, Jesus stays two days longer and many are converted, claiming in verse 42, "We no longer believe just because of what you said; now we have heard for ourselves, and we know that this man really is the Savior of the world" (John 4:42).

> "He chose the lowly things of this world and the despised things— and the things that are not—to nullify the things that are, so that no one may boast before him." (1 Corinthians 1:28–29)

What a glorious end to the story! The final words are "We know that this man really is the Savior of the world." What if your words sowed seeds that caused others to seek out the Savior? What if listeners "heard" Jesus speak and teach through time spent in His word and became convinced that *this man really is the Savior of the world!*

In His encounter with the Samaritan woman, Jesus broke racial, social, cultural, and religious rules. He shouldn't have spoken to a *Samaritan* woman *alone*, and certainly not about *religious topics*.[8] And yet in this encounter, Jesus took that which was despised and weak and used it to bring wisdom to others, as the Samaritan woman becomes one of the first missionaries in the Gospels!

Jesus' Words in Action: In what way does Jesus seek you out? In what ways are you surprised when He knows so much more than you want Him to know? How is this almost reassuring? Today, how can you unburden yourself by talking to Him?

What is your food today? What is the Father's will for you today? In what ways do you plant seeds, or perhaps tend the seeds others have planted? How is your place of work a harvest field? Who are your modern-day Samaritans? Which of your acquaintances needs to learn about Jesus from you?

Wednesday: Two Stories—Throwing Stones and The Widow at Nain

People in glass houses shouldn't throw stones. We've all heard that saying and know it means others may attack us if we attack them. Another well-known quote is, "If any one of you is without sin, let him be the first to throw a stone. . ." (John 8:7).

Stoning was the punishment for adultery. The woman of John 8 was caught in the act of adultery, and she would pay the price.

📖 Read John 7:53—8:11 to learn more about throwing stones.

In this passage, Jesus spends time on the Mount of Olives before dawn. Can we assume Jesus is beginning His day in prayer? Other times, Jesus comes to the temple courts and begins teaching the many gathered around him at dawn.

1. You've seen how Jesus treated the Samaritan woman. How is Jesus' response to the Pharisees and teachers of the law different (verses 3–5)?

_____

_____

The adultery concern levied by the Pharisees is sexist: only one partner is brought in. For the woman to have been caught in the act may mean the event is a setup.[9] If she were a known prostitute, that would not have been difficult. But the purpose of bringing her to the *temple* is to trap Jesus. Jesus' response is simple and in two parts: actions followed by words.

2. Consider what Jesus draws on the ground in verse 6. What do you think he writes?

_____

_____

3. What kind of questions do you think the Pharisees ask him (verse 7)?

_____

_____

> "If any one of you is without sin, let him be the first to throw a stone at her." (John 8:7b)
>
>

4. How does his audible response apply to the times you might accuse, condemn or gossip about another person?

_____

5. After Jesus resumes his writing, what happens to the accusers?

_____

_____

Something is written on the ground. Is it the sins of those

gathered or perhaps an I.O.U. for the woman's salvation? We don't know, but she now stands alone with Jesus, who straightens to a standing position and inquires about her accusers. She responds that no one is left to condemn her. Although her accusers drop their stones and leave, the weight of her sin remains until Jesus says, "Then neither do I condemn you. Go now and leave your life of sin" (verse 11). She doesn't know that He will take on the weight of her sins and die on the cross. Though we often memorize John 3:16 about *why* God sent His Son, verse 17 emphasizes that He did not send His son to judge.

Jesus' Words in Action: Do you help those with problems, or are you prone to judge and stone them? Do you condemn, or do you bring people to a saving knowledge of Jesus? In what ways can you be more Christ-like in your daily encounters so that you aren't like the Pharisees? If someone came into your church with a history like the adulterous woman, the Samaritan woman, or a greedy tax collector, could you respond like Jesus?

> "For God did not send his Son into the world to condemn the world, but to save the world through him." (John 3:17)

Jesus sends the adulterous woman out with a command to "Go now and leave your life of sin" (verse 11). I cannot imagine this woman returning to her former life after being *saved* by the Messiah. Though it's still impossible to live a perfect life, we are led by the One who is perfect, loving, holy, and forgiving. Doesn't this inspire you to present yourselves as holy? It does me (Romans 12:1–2)!

If you can relate to this woman and are looking for a fresh start, Jesus gives you the inspiration to step out and claim it. He wants this woman—and all of us—to begin again. Believe in Him, accept Him as your Savior, and ask for forgiveness. Find a non-pharisaical church that can embrace and disciple a new believer. Go now and leave your sin. Become a new creation in Christ! (2 Corinthians 5:17).

Note: Some scholars doubt whether John wrote John 7:53—8:11. Early manuscripts do not include this passage, and the other Gospel writers do not cover the event. Because it is in the Bible, we are covering this woman's encounter with Jesus.

Now let's learn about the widow of Nain, whose *heart* catches Jesus' attention.

📖 Read Luke 7:11–17 (the widow at Nain).

Place yourself again in AD 30. As a woman of that time, you may have heard that Jesus heals. You may have heard the Samaritan woman at the well explain that Jesus is the Messiah. But today, for the first time, Jesus reveals His power over death.

After Jesus performs a long-distance healing of the centurion's servant, He leaves Capernaum and encounters a lowly widow in the village of Nain, ten miles from his native Nazareth. (Refer to map on page 16.) Jesus' large crowd meets the widow's large crowd to make quite a gathering of witnesses.

1. What three facts do you know about the woman Jesus meets (verse 12)?

_____

_____

2. How does Jesus react to her (verse 13)?

_____

_____

Luke is the only Gospel writer who records this scene. Why? Perhaps he was a sensitive doctor who considered certain situations more important. Perhaps each Gospel writer's emphasis gives us a clearer view of Christ's life.

If Jesus said to me, "Don't cry" (Luke 7:13), I'd probably cry harder. There are times I'm barely holding it together and then someone lovingly says, "I care." Compassion, sympathy, and empathy bring me to tears. Oh, the sadness of that poor, lonely widow who has lost her only son. She now has no provider or companion. All hope must be lost except for the arrival of a man whose heart goes out to her. Can she comprehend how dearly He loves her? Can she fathom how deeply He wants her to have life and to have it abundantly?

My friend, Jesus would meet you at the gate, too. When all hope is lost, He sees your trouble, and He does care. He'll meet you anywhere, and He'll hear your cries.

What do you suppose the crowds do in reaction? The men

carrying the coffin have stopped their progress. Jesus' words are to the point, "Young man, I say to you, get up!" (Luke 7:14). Does that sound ridiculous? Jesus talking to a dead man? But what happens? The dead man (Note: *dead* man) sits up and talks. He doesn't mumble or cough; he *talks*.

_____

_____

3. What do you suppose the "dead man" says?

_____

_____

4. Who do you suppose the "dead man" sees surrounding him?

_____

> *If you stood in Jesus' crowd, how would you feel about your teacher? If you were a mourner in the other crowd, what would you be thinking about Him?*

Two separate crowds of men and women watch as Jesus gives "him back to his mother." What a gift! She may not even have asked Him for this, but Jesus knows her need, he understands her sorrow, and grieves to the point of responding to her pain.

This is one of the few instances of Jesus raising someone from the dead. We will see the raising of Jairus' daughter, and later Lazarus. But this is the first recorded time that Jesus resurrects a person from the dead.

5. What is the crowd's reaction (verse 16)?

_____

_____

6. Who do they claim Jesus is (verse 16)?

_____

_____

They even explain, "God has come to help his people" (verse 16). Indeed. But did any of them really understand that He truly is more than a prophet? Can they fathom that Jesus is "God with us," Immanuel? Do the disciples even grasp that this man is really *God on earth* to help his people?

6. What is the ultimate consequence of this resurrection (verse 17)?

A friend of mine suddenly lost her four-year-old daughter to Strep A virus. There was nothing Lori or the doctors could have done to save little Katie. As her daughter was ushered into heaven, Lori came to know Jesus Christ as her savior. She compares herself with the widow of Nain. "My first instinct wasn't to begin crying out to God— I didn't really know Him at that time. He saw *me* and had compassion!" Jesus met her at the gate with His presence and peace. As Lori dealt with Katie's death, she came to new life in Jesus.

> Two separate crowds witness the compassion of Christ as well as His resurrection power.

Lori wonders if the Gentiles to whom Luke writes were similarly touched by the widow's story. She says, "This could speak to the Gentiles who hadn't been raised with the Scriptures and who wouldn't necessarily call out to the God of the Jews. This would be like many of us today, the unsaved, who really don't know *Who* to call out to. But Jesus comes and meets us anyway."

> "The LORD is close to the brokenhearted and saves those who are crushed in spirit." (Psalm 34:18)
>

One good-bye became the beginning of a hello in eternity; for Lori knows that one day she will meet Katie again. Though Katie wasn't raised from the dead, in effect, Lori was. Two weeks after Katie's death, Lori began sharing her story. Years later, the Lord blessed Lori and her husband with the surprise of Benjamin, Katie's little brother.

Jesus' Words in Action: No one needed to tell Jesus the story of the woman of Nain. He knew she had lost her husband and her son and was now alone. He met her needs even though she didn't ask for help. Are you going through something alone? Do you feel like Jesus doesn't notice? Do you feel you've been stripped of what you love and have nothing left? Just when you're leaving, Jesus is coming. Meet Him at the gate, and let Him take care of you. He *does* notice loneliness, death, and sorrow, and He *does* want to respond.

Do you know someone who needs the Savior's comfort? In prayer today, ask the Lord to place someone on your heart. Be the hands and heart of Jesus and reach out at the gate with words of comfort and love.

Thursday: A Sinful Woman Anoints Jesus

Each of the Gospels tells of Jesus being anointed by a woman (Matthew 26:7–13; Mark 14:3–9; Luke 7:36–50; John 12:1–8). Some readers interpret the four passages as being three *different* women with Matthew and Mark covering the same anointing. Some believe that *all* of the passages are about the *same* woman. Some believe that *three* of the passages refer to Mary of Bethany, while the other refers to an unnamed sinner. Though there are many similarities in the passages, the differences in the Luke 7 passage lead me to believe that this anointing is different from the anointing Jesus receives near His death. I am inclined to read the four passages as at least two separate accounts: the sinner woman anointing Jesus early in His ministry, and Mary, sister of Martha, anointing Jesus the week before His crucifixion.

But before we look at the passage, let's remove misconceptions we may have. This Luke passage never names the sinner woman as Mary Magdalene. Much has been attributed to Mary Magdalene that may not belong to her. Tomorrow we will explore what the Bible *does* say about her in depth. Suffice it to say, this woman of Luke 7 loved and anointed Jesus and remains *unnamed* but not *unloved* by the Lord.

Read Luke 7:36–50.

Consider the house and host.

1. Who is hosting the event? In what ways is the woman a stark contrast to the host?

_____

_____

A Pharisee hosting Jesus was revolutionary enough! But now a woman enters his home. Culturally this just did not happen. Plus, what do we know about her? Not only is she sinful, she's led a sinful life *in that town.*

2. How might those in the house know of her past?

_____

3. List the actions she takes to honor Jesus (verses 38, 44–46).

_____

Are you surprised about her use of hair? Don't be. A master sometimes dried his hands on a servant's hair in the first century.[10] After walking in sandals through dusty streets, having His feet washed and massaged would have been customary and welcomed. At His entry, she honors Him as Lord in a way no one else did.

The perfume she carries is a costly, aromatic liquid made from the root of an Indian plant. The Old Testament refers to this substance in Song of Songs 1:12; 4:13, 14. She carries this perfume in an alabaster jar, a soft substance that looks like marble. Because alabaster boxes of this time often hold perfume, most containers filled with perfume are called alabaster whether they are or not. To release the perfume, the vessel has to be broken.[11]

> The jar has to be broken to release the sweet perfume. In what ways do we need to be broken to release our sweetness?

In AD 30, men do not talk to women in public, avoid touching women, and women do likewise. But Jesus does not recoil at the woman's touch. For Jesus to be anointed by a woman who was known to be sinful is culturally and religiously taboo. No self-respecting Pharisee would have allowed himself to be made ceremonially unclean by a known sinner.

4. You can almost hear the Pharisee's judgmental tone of voice. What is the response of the Pharisee, and to whom does he speak (verse 39)?

_____

_____

Jesus then responds to the Pharisee's grumbling by teaching with a parable, a beautiful story about two men owing money and a moneylender who forgives them. The one man's debt is five hundred denarii (500 days' wages) and the other owes fifty denarii (50 days' wages). Thus, one man is forgiven about seventeen months' income, while the other is forgiven about two months' worth.

Jesus draws a parallel: the woman who anointed him is the debtor forgiven five hundred denarii, and the Pharisee is the debtor forgiven one-tenth that amount. Jesus contrasts what she has done for Him with what the Pharisee failed to do. She treated Him like a king, literally. To anoint a king's head with oil is similar to a current-day crowning (1 Samuel 16:13; 2 Samuel 5:3; 1 Kings 1:39).

5. As Jesus relates this story, how do you think this woman feels? In her humbled position, tears streaming down her face, what is going through her mind?

_____

_____

6. Write down Jesus' response in verse 47.

_____

This woman lavishly loves the One who changed her life. We don't hear that she *asks* for forgiveness, but her loving and respectful actions *beg* for it. Jesus knows her heart and says, "Your faith has saved you; go in peace" (verse 50).

7. Describe the change in this woman's feelings and life from the time she enters the home until she leaves.

_____

_____

What about us? Do we really understand the difference Jesus made in coming to earth for us? Can we speak about a difference?

_____

_____

8. How is she similar, yet different, from the woman at the well?

_____

_____

9. How is Jesus' response to her similar to His response to the adulterous woman?

_____

_____

Jesus' Words in Action: Faith, forgiveness, and healing have been linked throughout Jesus' ministry. What about in your life? How many of us walk around with chips on our shoulders? How many of us are stingy at showing love and forgiveness? Similarly, how many of us are so slow to say "I'm sorry" that we walk around unforgiven?

Are you in need of forgiveness from God or from your neighbor, friends, or family? If there is a long-outstanding wrong, it's time to ask forgiveness. Or has someone wronged you? Has the debt of fifty denarii driven a spike of anger, bitterness, and resentment into your heart? Is it time to forgive the debt of fifty denarii you feel is owed to you since Jesus has forgiven you of so much more?

Jesus exalts this woman. She is remembered. Because He sets this up as such a positive example, we need to study this story and incorporate her good qualities in our lives.

What can we learn from this woman's act of worship? How can we emulate it today? When you honor the Lord, do you lavishly love Him by giving of your time, talents, and finances? Do you reveal that you've been loved much and forgiven much?

Friday: The Real Mary Magdalene (Part I)

One year I was asked to play Mary, Mother of Jesus in our local passion play. But later, the director asked if I could switch and play a different Mary: Mary Magdalene. My preschooler was disappointed. She felt hurt that I was demoted to playing a "crazy lady."

I'm not sure where my daughter came up with that idea, but misconceptions about Mary Magdalene abound. Whole books have been written about this woman. Uncovering the real Mary is the subject of liberal speculation as well as conservative scholarship. (If you desire additional background, see the endnotes for sources of research.)

Scholarship from the Word of God is our focus for today. The first mention of Mary Magdalene is in Luke 8:1–3, where she is listed among the women disciples. In many cases, she is listed first and appears to be a leader among the women. Matthew and Mark record that certain women followed and cared for Jesus' needs (Matthew 27:55–56; Mark 15:40–41). Doctor Luke records the following:

> *What's your first reaction to Mary Magdalene?*

> *After this, Jesus traveled about from one town and village to another, proclaiming the good news of the kingdom*

of God. The Twelve were with him, and also some women who had been cured of evil spirits and diseases: Mary (called Magdalene) *from whom seven demons had come out; Joanna the wife of Cuza, the manager of Herod's household; Susanna; and many others. These women were helping to support them out of their own means. (Luke 8:1–3)*

1. Twelve male disciples followed Jesus. Who else was there?

_____

_____

_____

A group of women with similar backgrounds are hearing the stories of Jesus, believing, and committing their lives and their finances to His work. They may have temporarily or on a day-to-day basis left their families and their homes to follow Him. Some have been forgiven much, so they forgive much.[12] Mary is the leader of these women. But before we say who she *is*, let's talk about who she is *not*. Much of what we consider about her is myth.

Specifically, the Bible does *not* say Mary Magdalene is a prostitute. The Bible does *not* say that she is the sinner woman who anoints Jesus. As a matter of fact, Liz Curtis Higgs' fascinating book *Mad Mary: A Bad Girl from Magdala* points out that in Luke 7 the sinner who anoints Jesus is *unnamed*, whereas at the beginning of Luke 8, Mary Magdalene is introduced completely unrelated to the previous passage. Jesus tells the sinner woman of Luke 7 to go in peace, not to come follow Him.[13]

Because artists have long depicted a repentant and worshipful Mary Magdalene, this is the picture we are left with. Another false picture comes from the portrayal in film and literature that Mary Magdalene is the wife of Jesus and mother of His child. Now remove artistic interpretation and previous misconceptions to focus on what the Bible says about the woman who is second only to the Mother of Jesus in New Testament coverage. Hold onto this one fact: Mary follows Jesus to the cross and beyond. She is so changed by His power to transform that she has faith when others walk away.

The Mary confusion is complicated by the many other

Marys discussed in the New Testament. This list may help you sort them out as we study:

The *Other* New Testament Marys

Mary of Nazareth, mother of Jesus

Mary, the wife of Clopas (John 19:25)

Mary, mother of James and Joses (Matthew 27:56; Mark 15:40; Luke 24:10)

Mary of Bethany, sister of Lazarus and Martha (Luke 10:39)

Mary of Jerusalem, mother of Mark (Acts 12:12)

Mary of Rome (aide to Paul, Romans 16:6)

The *other* Mary (Matthew 27:61; 28:1)

While other Marys are defined by their families, Mary Magdalene is defined by her hometown of Magdala.[14] The Greek form of Magdalene is *Migdol* or *watchtower*.[15]

In AD 30 Magdala is a trading village on the Sea of Galilee (see map on p. 16). Not only is it the center of trade in salt fish, material, and agriculture, it also is a juncture of religions and customs represented by the Jewish and Hellenistic faiths.[16] Thus, Magdala feels the oppression, repression, and violence of Roman occupation.[17]

2. Look back at Luke 8:1–3. What do we know about the backgrounds of these female followers? How has Jesus touched their lives?

_____

_____

Liz Curtis Higgs explains,

He healed them, delivered them, saved them, empowered them. And though it's not recorded in Scripture, he may have called these women to share the gospel publicly as well. It's clear he counted them among his closest disciples. He gave their lives meaning in a culture that did not always value women.[18]

3. If we transferred Mary Magdalene's life to the screen, what scenes would be missing? In other words, what more would you like to know about her?

_____

_____

According to Luke 8, at some point in Mary's life, seven demons entered her. Demonology was very real in New Testament times. In *Mad Mary*, Liz Curtis Higgs speculates that some may doubt the existence of demons. However, she points out the following three facts:

1. Jesus himself acknowledges the existence of demons and evil spirits (Matthew 12:28; Luke 11:24).

2. Jesus speaks to demons (Mark 8:31–32; Mark 9:25).

3. The demons speak back to him (Luke 4:41). [19]

Besides, why would Jesus spend any of His precious time casting out something that doesn't exist? (Matthew 8:28–34; 12:22–32; Mark 3:22–27; 5:1–20; Luke 8:26–39; 11:14–23) The demons often understand who Jesus is and believe in Him. If ever there was a time when Satan should have been fighting, it was when God came to earth.

Wouldn't it be nice to see a "before and after" picture? Though the disciples may have witnessed Mary Magdalene's deliverance from demon oppression, it's not recorded. If you need to get an idea what the "before" picture might have looked like, flip to Luke 4:35 to see Jesus cast out a demon. Luke 8:26–39 and Mark 5:1–20 also describe a naked, demon-possessed, previously chained man living in the tombs. The demon-possessed man has broken free of his chains and "been driven by the demon into solitary places" (Luke 8:29). "No one was strong enough to subdue him" (Mark 5:4). Night and day the man cries out and cuts himself with stones. The evil spirit in him has seized him many times. When Jesus arrives, He gives the demons permission to enter two thousand pigs. The pigs rush off a steep bank and drown.

What happens when demons leave a person? There is instant change that all can see.

The people become so afraid, they ask Jesus to leave. The healed man begs to go with Jesus, but Jesus has a mission and purpose for this liberated man. " 'Return home and tell how much God has done for you.' So the man went away and told all over town how much Jesus had done for him" (Luke 8:39).

Based on the unattractive picture of the demon-possessed man, maybe we don't really want to see Mary Magdalene's "before" picture.[20] I can't presume what Mary's life was like prior to meeting Jesus, but if being possessed in body, mind, and personality by seven demons is anything like this man's torment and anguish, we know that Mary's life must have been hell on earth. Is it any wonder she freely follows the One who has liberated her? Jesus has a plan and a purpose for her life: follow, learn, and lead.

The Gospel writers include her background because it's important. So is yours. Your past may give you the background to make you a leader, counselor, or teacher. Your past reveals where you came from *before* Christ and how He has *transformed* you.

5. Considering the background information above, list words to describe Mary Magdalene's situation prior to meeting Jesus.

_____

_____

Mary chooses to follow Jesus. From town to town, she listens to Him, watches Him heal, and helps support His ministry. During this time she is a part of His inner circle of disciples. How do we know this? Let's jump way ahead to resurrection day and Mary Magdalene's encounter with the angel at the empty tomb, which we will study at length in Week 7. In *Mary Magdalene: Beyond the Myth*, Esther De Boer points out that the angel reminds the women that they had already heard Jesus tell them He would rise from the dead.[21]

> "They found the man from whom the demons had gone out, sitting at Jesus' feet, dressed and in his right mind." (Luke 8:35)
>

> *In their fright the women bowed down with their faces to the ground, but the men said to them, "Why do you look for the living among the dead? He is not here; he has risen! Remember how he told you, while he was still with you in Galilee: 'The Son of Man must be delivered into the hands of sinful men, be crucified and on the third*

day be raised again.' " Then they remembered his words. (Luke 24:5–8)

They *remembered* Jesus' words because they had been there *in person* when He prophesied. When did He say it? De Boer encourages us to go back to Luke 9:18–22, which describes Jesus praying in private with His disciples nearby.

> *Once when Jesus was praying in private and his disciples were with him, he asked them, "Who do the crowds say I am?" They replied, "Some say John the Baptist; others say Elijah; and still others, that one of the prophets of long ago has come back to life." "But what about you?" he asked. "Who do you say I am?"*
>
> *Peter answered, "The Christ of God." Jesus strictly warned them not to tell this to anyone. And he said, "The Son of Man must suffer many things and be rejected by the elders, chief priests and teachers of the law, and he must be killed and on the third day be raised to life." (Luke 9:18–22)*

In other words, De Boer concludes, "The women belong among those disciples who were evidently allowed to be with Jesus even when he withdrew into solitude to pray. The women belong among the disciples who hear things and are told things by Jesus which must remain hidden from others."[22]

This author also speculates that Mary follows because "She had grown up in a city in which the Roman occupation, the opposition to it and the suffering which that brought were tangible. That could have made her receptive precisely to the nonviolent, the spiritual and the healing element of the kingdom of God as this took shape in Jesus."[23] Perhaps the diversity of culture and faith in Mary's hometown of Magdala made her more receptive to the idea that Jesus came for all.[24]

But Mary doesn't just love Jesus' healing touch, and His teaching. Mary *loves Jesus.* She honors Him and cherishes Him. Though there is much more to be learned from Mary Magdalene, we're going to move on to other subjects until weeks seven and eight, when we examine her becoming the first witness to the resurrection. She has so much more to tell!

Jesus' Words in Action: Mary Magdalene is a model in so

many ways. She supported Jesus, supported His ministry, and led women. Obviously, Jesus transformed her life. But you, too, can be changed by Jesus' touch. Do you let Him change you in dramatic as well as in quiet and gentle ways? Could you lead other women by your example?

Saturday: "What Wondrous Love Is This?"

Scripture: "But God demonstrates his own love for us in this: While we were still sinners, Christ died for us." (Romans 5:8)

Why did God send His Son? Love. What caused Jesus to die? Love. What drew Mary near the cross? Love. Philip Yancey writes about the true power of love, "Although power can force obedience, only love can summon a response of love, which is the one thing God wants from us and the reason he created us."[25]

Today let's sing the Celtic American folk hymn "What Wondrous Love is This" written in a minor key with a major message. Sing it in praise of the *wondrous* love shown on that *wondrous* cross. Note the triumphant, victorious third and fourth verses. What unity and joy we have in Christ!

"What Wondrous Love Is This?"

What wondrous love is this, O my soul, O my soul!
What wondrous love is this, O my soul!
What wondrous love is this that caused the Lord of bliss
To bear the dreadful curse for my soul, for my soul,
To bear the dreadful curse for my soul.

When I was sinking down, sinking down, sinking down
When I was sinking down, sinking down;
When I was sinking down beneath God's righteous frown,
Christ laid aside His crown for my soul
Christ laid aside His crown for my soul.

To God and to the Lamb I will sing, I will sing;
To God and to the Lamb I will sing;
To God and to the Lamb who is the great "I Am,"
While millions join the theme, I will sing, I will sing;
While millions join the theme, I will sing.

And when from death I'm free, I'll sing on, I'll sing on,
And when from death I'm free, I'll sing on;
And when from death I'm free, I'll sing and joyful be,
And through eternity I'll sing on, I'll sing on,
And through eternity I'll sing on.

Response: *Thank you, dear Lamb of God, for bearing the dreadful curse and laying aside Your crown for me. You are the great I Am. May I never doubt Your claims and Your promises. I will lift up my voice and sing unto God and to the Lamb!*

Today, using words based on Ephesians 3, pray for someone you want to understand the fullness of God's wondrous love.

"I pray that out of God's glorious riches God may strengthen _____ with power through His Spirit in _____'s inner being, so that Christ may dwell in _____'s heart through faith. And I pray that _____, being rooted and established in love, may have power, together with all the saints, to grasp how wide and long and high and deep is the love of Christ, and to know this love that surpasses knowledge—that _____ may be filled to the measure of all the fullness of God." (based on Ephesians 3:16–19)

Sunday: "I Am Thine O Lord"

> God said to Moses, "**I AM** WHO **I AM**. This is what you are to say to the Israelites: '**I AM** has sent me to you.'" (Exodus 3:14)
>
>

Scripture: "Near the cross of Jesus stood his mother, his mother's sister, Mary the wife of Clopas, and Mary Magdalene." (John 19:25)

Are you beginning to grasp what drew the women to the cross despite their sadness, fear, and risk to their lives? Love. In 1875, another woman comprehended that kind of love and the longing to draw near to the cross. Fanny Crosby had been blind due to medical errors since she was six weeks old, but in her blindness, she could still long to be near the cross and Jesus' bleeding side.

Draw me nearer, nearer, nearer blessed Lord to the cross where Thou hast died

Draw me nearer, nearer, nearer, blessed Lord, to thy precious, bleeding side.

"I am Thine O Lord" is but one of her eight thousand hymns. (That's after a late start in her forties!) You may remember some of her other hymns, "Near the Cross" and the appropriately titled "All the Way My Savior Leads Me." One hymn written at the age of 71 begins, "And I shall **see** Him face to face, and tell the story—Saved by Grace."

Her sightlessness brought on a deeper insight. When pitied by a clergyman, she explained she would have chosen to be blind, "Because when I get to heaven, the first sight that shall ever gladden my eyes will be that of my Savior!"[26] What a moment that must have been when she first saw Jesus! Oh that my eyes would not be distracted by the glitter of the world and would instead only long to see my Savior's face! May her *song* be your *prayer* today.

"I Am Thine O Lord"

I am Thine, O Lord I have heard Thy voice—And it told Thy love to me;
But I long to rise in the arms of faith and be closer drawn to Thee.
Consecrate me now to Thy service, Lord, by the power of grace divine
Let my soul look up with a steadfast hope and my will be lost in Thine.

O the pure delight of a single hour that before Thy throne I spend
When I kneel in prayer and with Thee, my God, I commune as friend with friend.

There are depths of love that I cannot know till I cross the narrow sea;
There are heights of joy that I may not reach till I rest in peace with Thee.

Chorus:
Draw me nearer, nearer blessed Lord to the cross where Thou hast died
Draw me nearer, nearer, nearer, blessed Lord, to thy precious, bleeding side.

Prayer: *I am Thine, O Lord. I long to hear Thy voice today. I know You love me. Consecrate me to Your service. May I spend time communing with You as friend to friend. I love You Jesus.*

> Oh that my eyes would not be distracted by the glitter of the world and would instead only long to see my Savior's face!

Works Cited

1. Deffinbaugh, Bob, Th.M, "The Manifestation of Messiah to the Samaritan Woman (John 4:1–42)," http://www.bible.org.

2. Richards, Sue and Larry, *Every Woman in the Bible* (Nashville, TN: Thomas Nelson, 1999), 160.

3. Deffinbaugh, http://www.bible.org.

4. Ibid.

5. Ibid.

6. Ray Vander Laan and Focus on the Family Video (That the World May Know Series), *Faith Lessons on the Life and Ministry of the Messiah: Living Water* (Grand Rapids, MI: Zondervan, 1996, 1998), Volume 3, Video 2.

7. Deffinbaugh, http://www.bible.org.

8. Ibid.

9. Richards, 180.

10. Higgs, Liz Curtis, *Mad Mary: A Bad Girl from Magdala, Transformed at His Appearing* (Colorado Springs, CO: WaterBrook Press, 2001), 143.

11. *Easton's Bible Dictionary* in Accordance Bible software. CD-ROM, version 5.7. Oak Tree Software, Inc.

12. De Boer, Esther, *Mary Magdalene: Beyond the Myth* (Harrisburg, PA: Trinity Press International, 1996), 31.

13. Higgs, 144.

14. De Boer, 55.

15. Higgs, 150.

16. Deen, Edith, *All of the Women of the Bible* (New York: Harper and Brothers, 1955), 202.

17. De Boer, 29–30.

18. Higgs, 182.

19. Ibid.,161.

20. Ibid.,170.

21. De Boer, 37.

22. Ibid.

23. Ibid., 41.

24. Ibid.

25. Yancey, Philip, *The Jesus I Never Knew* (Grand Rapids, MI: Zondervan, 1995), 78.

26. Osbeck, Kenneth W., *Amazing Grace: 366 Inspiring Hymn Stories for Daily Devotions.*

WEEK THREE:

TRAVELING WITH JESUS

Six Women Touched by Him

Monday: Jesus Heals in Capernaum
A Story within a Story

This week we will meet a few more women touched by Jesus. Today, place yourself in the crowd of Jesus' followers and witness a story within a story.

The people have heard that Jesus heals and casts out demons; now whenever Jesus arrives, crowds gather to listen to Him and beg for healing. What image do you have of Him? What feelings come over you as you realize how much He loves children, women, sinners, and the sick?

Three *unnamed* but not *untouched* women meet Jesus. Matthew, Mark, and Luke all record this story, but we'll focus on Mark's story, enhanced with details from Matthew and Luke.

📖 Read Mark 5:21–43 (Matthew 9:18–26; Luke 8:41–56).

1. What is Jairus' career? Why is this significant (Mark 5:22)?

_____

_____

2. How does Jairus approach Jesus (Mark 5:22)?

_____

_____

The accounts differ slightly about whether his only daughter is dying or has already died (Matthew 9:18; Luke 8:42). Inserted into Jairus' daughter's story is a woman who is not *twelve years old*, but who has struggled for *twelve years* with bleeding.

3. What has the woman lost because of her poor health (Mark 5:26)?

Remember our study in Week One about laws for women during menstruation? This woman is ritually unclean and should not be touched—not before, during, or immediately after her menstrual cycle. She is not to worship, enter the temple, or join a group of people. She can't even be with her husband, light the candles on Sabbath, or join in the Passover meal.[1] She most certainly should not be reaching out to touch someone's clothes.

Despite the religious and cultural taboo, this woman touches the edge or fringe of Christ's cloak, the tassels (Luke 8:44).

4. Using this passage from the Old Testament book of Numbers, underline the purpose for tassels on garments.

> *The LORD said to Moses, "Speak to the Israelites and say to them: 'Throughout the generations to come you are to make tassels on the corners of your garments, with a blue cord on each tassel. You will have these tassels to look at and so you will remember all the commands of the LORD, that you may obey them and not prostitute yourselves by going after the lusts of your own hearts and eyes. Then you will remember to obey all my commands and will be consecrated to your God. I am the LORD your God, who brought you out of Egypt to be your God. I am the LORD your God.' " (Numbers 15:37–41)*

Tassels also had other meanings. The five knots signified the five books of Moses and God's Covenant with His people. The four spaces between represented the four consonant letters of God's name: *YHWH*. The tassels reminded the wearer to keep all 613 laws and to serve the One God. It was believed that touching the tassels could produce forgiveness and healing.[2]

Think about the hemorrhaging woman. Does she know of Jesus' other healings? Does she long to be touched by another person? Does she fear the scorn of those around her as she wriggles through the crowd? Does she hide her face lest she be discovered? Does she hesitate before grabbing the tassels?

5. How does the woman approach Jesus at first (Mark 5:27)?

_____

_____

6. How does Jesus respond to her touch (Mark 5:30)?

_____

_____

Jesus doesn't want her life to be defined by her illness. She may be like a shepherd's reed, broken and unable to play a tune. She may be like a smoldering wick unable to burn, but He sees that her life has light and a future. He will bring hope not only to the nations but also *specifically* to *her*.[3] Her bleeding stops immediately and she is "freed from her suffering" (Mark 5:29).

> "A bruised reed he will not break, and a smoldering wick he will not snuff out, till he leads justice to victory. In his name the nations will put their hope." (Matthew 12:20–21)

Though He knows the answer, Jesus asks, "Who is the one who touched Me?" (Luke 8:45). Still, Peter gives a quick response, "Good grief, there are so many people pushing and shoving. Of course someone touched you!" (Ann's version of Luke 8:45) But Jesus persists, "Someone touched me; I know that power has gone out from me" (Luke 8:46).

7. How do the disciples react to Jesus' question (Mark 5:31)?

_____

_____

8. How does the woman now approach Jesus (Mark 5:33)?

_____

_____

9. Meanwhile, what do you think Jairus is thinking? Remember that he is a synagogue ruler and she is a hemorrhaging woman!

_____

_____

10. What does Jesus say to her? "_____, your _____ has _____ you. ___ in _____ and be _____ from your _____" (Mark 5:34).

In *The Jesus I Never Knew*, Philip Yancey makes this observation about Jesus' nurturing response to the unclean woman.

> Jesus was often "moved by compassion," and in New Testament times that very word was used maternally to express what a mother feels for her child in her womb. Jesus went out of his way to embrace the unloved and unworthy, the folks who matter not at all to the rest of society—they embarrass us, we wish they'd go away—to prove that even "nobodies" matter infinitely to God. One unclean woman, too shy and full of shame to approach Jesus face-to-face, grabbed his robe hoping he would not notice. He did notice. She learned, like so many other "nobodies," that you cannot easily escape Jesus' gaze.[4]

Jesus loved the unlovely, the rejected, those who didn't fit in the crowd, and even those who weren't allowed to be there. Jesus calls this unnamed woman *"daughter."* What a gentle and loving term from a fatherly Jesus.

By verse 35, we move back to story #1 and another father and daughter. However, when someone arrives from Jairus' house, they all hear it's too late for the daughter of Jairus. "'Your daughter is dead,' he said. 'Don't bother the teacher any more'" (Luke 8:49). Now what do you think Jairus is thinking and feeling? Does Jairus have any knowledge of Jesus' raising the widow woman's only son from the dead in the village of Nain, twenty miles away? Is Jairus reassured by the healing he has just witnessed?

Whatever is going through his head, he must see that Jesus is the answer and has the answer. "Don't be afraid; just believe, and she will be healed" (Luke 8:50).

Matthew 9:23 reveals that when Jesus enters Jairus' home, he finds flute players and a noisy crowd. This disorder, weeping, and wailing is customary at funerals, but Jesus wants it stopped and His comments about their display make them laugh.

11. Why does Jesus allow only Peter, James, and John, brother of James, to witness the scene?

_____

_____

Only the father and mother and Jesus' companions are allowed to enter the child's room. The professional mourners who mocked Jesus will miss out on the miracle.

Let's bring up the lights on the two unnamed females in the room: Jairus' daughter and wife. Although we have no description of the girls' mother, I have an inkling about what she's feeling. When a child of mine has a high fever, I want to be close by.

As a young mom, I feared leaving my children. I felt as though nothing terrible could happen to them as long as I was there. As I'd return home, I'd look up towards our house on the hill and expect to see an emergency vehicle in the driveway.

And so it doesn't surprise me that it's the dad who goes out to find the man they've heard can cast out demons and heal. What is Mom thinking while she helplessly watches her daughter slip away? What is she thinking when the mourners come to grieve at her daughter's death? What is she thinking when she sees Jesus take her little girl's hand and say, "Talitha koum! (which means, 'Little girl, I say to you, get up!')" (Mark 5:41).

Characteristically, Mark translates for his Gentile readers and says *immediately* the girl rose and began to walk, astonishing her mother and father.

12. Why do you think Jesus tells the parents not to tell anyone about this?

_____

_____

13. What might the mother be feeling? What might the daughter be feeling?

_____

_____

Jesus then says the child should be given something to eat. What a reassurance it is that their daughter needs energy because life has returned to her body. If Jesus told me my child needed to eat, I'd start cooking! Divine miracles don't replace common care. Talk about knowing a 12-year-old's physical as well as spiritual needs!

Jesus' Words in Action: Who are we like in this story? Are we like Jairus who runs to find Jesus to help with his problem?

Do we come forward on our knees, asking for what we need? Or do we call friends on the telephone or E-mail acquaintances with our concerns?

In what ways do we need to be more like the hemorrhaging woman who touched Jesus? What did it take for her to wriggle through the crowd and reach for the tassel on Jesus' robe? She touched the master because of her courage and faith.

Our lives may seem as though they've been hemorrhaging and that nothing can make us whole again. Things have gone wrong for so long, and so many have treated our sickness in so many different ways that we long to just grab onto Jesus. Can we come to Him in faith knowing that we are not *unnamed* and we are not *unloved?* Jesus loves the unlovely, the rejected, those who not only don't *fit in the crowd* but those who aren't even *allowed* to be there. He will feel our touch, and we will feel His power!

Tuesday: The Canaanite's Persistent Faith in Adversity

You've heard about the woman who reached out in faith and was healed. But have you ever reached out in faith to hear the answer "No" or "Wait?" Perhaps you're not even sure your request was heard. Should you persevere in prayer? Does Jesus desire persistence? Let's look at Jesus' teaching.

Not every woman who encountered Jesus had as gentle a reception as the woman who reached for his fringe. I'd almost rather leave this next story out of our study. Jesus doesn't come across quite as compassionate, gentle, and easily moved to heal. In fact, this incident makes me question His approachability. But difficult Bible passages often prompt the most questions and intrigue. Besides, *two* Gospel writers record the story. Obviously, the words from the Word are here to teach. Now it's up to us to glean the truth.

This woman is called a Syrophoenician—indicating she is from Phoenecia, specifically the region near Tyre and Sidon. Tyre is a commercial center, and Sidon is one of the oldest cities in the region. *Phoenecian* is the term Greeks used for Canaanite. Canaanites are descendants of Noah's son Ham, who had a son named Canaan. Canaan was cursed because of the sins of his father (see Genesis 9:22–27). At different times in history, Canaanites worshipped the sun god Baal, and idolatry was often prevalent in this region.

As a Gentile, this woman is not considered by the Jews to be worthy of anything. Yet Jesus is about to reveal some new rules.

This encounter comes after Jesus heals diseases and demoniacs, epileptics and paralytics, and teaches that the inside of a person is more important than the outside.

📖 Read Matthew 15:21–28 (also Mark 7:24–30).

1. An unnamed but not unknown woman comes to Jesus. Her little girl has an unclean spirit, a demon residing in her body. Write this woman's plea (Matthew 15:22).

_____

_____

_____

My first grader is afraid there might be somebody hiding in the attic at night. Each night we talk to her about how nobody could have slipped in and that Daddy and Mommy can keep her safe. At this point, however, rationalizing cannot relieve her of anxiety. I would gladly take on her fears to alleviate her burden, yet I feel helpless. This poor Gentile mother is experiencing something far worse. An evil spirit torments her little daughter. What anguish that would bring!

> "In fact, as soon as she heard about him, a woman whose little daughter was possessed by an evil spirit came and fell at his feet." (Mark 7:25)

2. What was Jesus' first response to the woman's heartfelt plea (Matthew 15:23)?

_____

_____

At first Jesus doesn't say anything (Matthew 15:23). What do we do when Jesus is silent? Quite frankly, at this point many of us would have given up. Some would have slinked back through the crowd, embarrassed and saddened. But a mother will do anything for a troubled child. What mother wouldn't jump in front of a bus if her child ran into a busy street? What mother wouldn't spend her life's savings on therapy or rehabilitation if her daughter were sick? The twenty-first century offers plenty of troubles for girls: anorexia, bulimia, premarital sex, drug abuse, alcohol abuse, cutting, sexual abuse; and without knowing Jesus, this world can seem like a very scary place for mothers. But knowing Jesus' love and knowing I can pray to Him gives me confidence and peace.

3. How do the disciples respond (Matthew 15:23)?

_____

_____

4. Jesus' next response in verse 24 seems strange. "I was sent only to the lost sheep of the house of Israel." What does He mean?

_____

_____

In John 10:16, Jesus reveals that He has come to bring in the *other* sheep. "I have other sheep that are not of this sheep pen. I must bring them also. They too will listen to my voice, and there shall be one flock and one shepherd" (John 10:16).

The woman's faith is great, and she listens to the voice of the Shepherd. Like most mothers, this Canaanite would not give up hope that her daughter would heal. She persists in the face of adversity. She cries out with the title, "Son of David"!

5. In Matthew 15:25, what is her next step?

_____

6. Beyond the love of her child, why would she persist? What encourages her faith in Jesus (verse 25)?

_____

_____

As if His silence and then restrictions were not enough, Jesus adds, "It is not good to take the children's bread and throw it to the dogs" (Matthew 15:26).

Maybe you're thinking Jesus now appears unapproachable. Why would He call this woman and her daughter *"dogs"*? Will the mother stick around for more? Bible Commentator Matthew Henry writes that this story teaches

> that there may be love in Christ's heart while there are frowns in his face; and it encourages us, though he seems ready to slay us, yet to trust in him. Those

whom Christ intends most to honour, he humbles to feel their own unworthiness. A proud, unhumbled heart would not have borne this; but she turned it into an argument to support her request.[5]

Let's look a bit at the translation. According to Ryrie, the children in the illustration are the lost sheep of Israel, and they must be fed before the dogs (Gentiles).[6]

Like the woman who grabs out in faith for the tassel on Jesus' robe, this mother reaches out again and again in words and argument.

7. What does she call Jesus this time? And whose table is she referring to (verse 27)?

_____

_____

8. In keeping with Jesus' analogy, what is she saying that Jesus should do for her daughter (verse 27)?

_____

_____

9. Why does Jesus now respond differently (verse 28)?

_____

_____

Jesus admires persistence. Consider Jesus' story from Luke 18:3–5 about the widow seeking justice. The woman's persistent knocking finally convinces the judge. If persistence is attractive, why do *we* give up so easily in the face of adversity?

10. Why is her daughter healed (Matthew 15:28)? In which previous healings have you seen Christ operate similarly?

_____

_____

11. How soon is her daughter healed (Matthew 15:28)?

_____

_____

Mark 7:29 adds further information when Jesus says, "For such a reply, you may go; the

> ### Words of Jesus:
>
> "Ask and it will be given to you; seek and you will find; knock and the door will be opened to you. For everyone who asks receives; he who seeks finds; and to him who knocks, the door will be opened." (Matthew 7:7–8)
>
>

demon has left your daughter."

Sometimes Jesus heals in the presence of the sick one; sometimes he heals from a long distance. The woman doesn't linger in doubt to continue the debate. She must be convinced and reassured. Though she doesn't see the immediate answer to her plea, she shows great faith. Does she *run* all the way home? Mark 7:30 reports that she returns home to find her daughter in bed, and the demon is gone.

I want to see blessed reconciliation and healing of their relationship. I want to see the mother and daughter in sweet conversation and communion. How does the mother explain the healing to her daughter?

Jesus' Words in Action: We don't know if the mother ever met Jesus again. The hike from Tyre to Jerusalem was long. But we do know this: Jesus promised to come to save more than just the Jewish race. Jesus came for all people and longs to answer persistent prayer. This woman is no doubt spending eternity with Jesus.

What about you? Is there something you've longed and prayed for? Have you felt like a dog that the master has not fed? Come in faith with your godly requests. Fall at His feet. Plead your case before the Master. Persist in prayer. He truly desires healing and reconciliation for families. I believe our God wants to answer the prayers of His children. He will give you more than scraps. He cares about your fears even more than your earthly parents. He loves you enough that He gave His life to reconcile you to your Father.

Wednesday: Mary and Martha
A Short Play in Three Acts (I and II)

For the next two days we'll read about two familiar women in an unfamiliar way. We'll study Mary and Martha and the rise in tension around Jerusalem. We will study their appearances as a play in three acts: "Hosting Jesus," "Death of Lazarus," and "Mary Anoints Jesus."

Consider these two unmarried sisters in light of their culture and time. They should have been married by the age of 13. Their father has probably died and passed the house on to his only son, Lazarus. Or Martha could have been a widow living in the home of her deceased husband. All that we know is that they are currently unmarried. In AD 30, their single status is looked down upon by many.[7]

This family plays a crucial role in the final weeks of Jesus' life on earth, because it is Jesus' raising Lazarus from the dead that further incites the religious leaders to arrest Him. Mary of Bethany's anointing of Jesus foreshadows Jesus' death and resurrection. Today we'll study two acts. Thursday's Act III is much shorter. Gauge your time accordingly.

Mary and Martha

As you study these two women, use this Venn diagram to compare and contrast them.

I've started it for you.

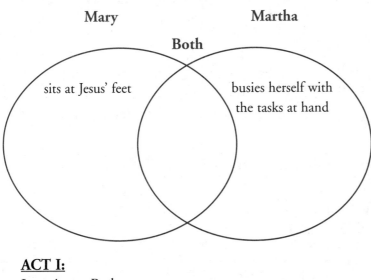

Mary   Martha

Both

sits at Jesus' feet

busies herself with the tasks at hand

ACT I:

Location: Bethany
Time: Months prior to death
Cast: _____
Title: _____

1. Read Luke 10:38–42, then fill in the cast list and title for Act I.

_____

2. What do you know about Martha from verse 38?

_____

_____

3. What troubles Martha most about the situation (verse 40)?

_____

_____

The woman's role is to serve in the kitchen, not to hang around with the guys, and most certainly not to be taught. But here we have Jesus breaking all the cultural rules by allowing a woman to sit at His feet and absorb His teaching. The *Torah* is for the sons and not for the daughters. One Rabbi of this time goes so far as to say that the words of the Torah should be burned rather than taught to women.[8] And yet, that's clearly not Jesus' perspective.

4. Write Jesus' response below, but instead of "*Martha, Martha,*" write in your *own* name.

_____

_____

5. Record differences and similarities in Mary and Martha in the diagram on page 65.

_____

_____

> *When are you more focused on your church work than on the Lord?*
>
> *When do you look at what others are doing instead of looking at your own heart?*
>
> *Do you know someone who is a Mary?*

6. What could you learn from the words of the Lord? In what areas are you:

distracted

_____

worried

_____

bothered

_____

7. If Jesus came to your house today, what would concern you most?
- the outward cleanliness of your home
- the way you look
- what you say to other family members
- the state of your heart
- whether you have a peaceful, loving home

To keep focused, I begin the day with a to-do list scribbled on paper to remind myself of all the things I need to get done. I love to scratch them off one by one. But what I often leave off the list are the most important:

- time in prayer with Jesus
- time in the Word
- pause for the loving little moments with my children
- pause to love my husband in tangible ways

These often don't make it onto the list because I want to finish what I can visibly see makes a difference. But my heart preparations *do* make a difference. The time spent with the Lord *does* impact the rest of my to-do list. What does your list look like for today? How can you put Jesus' words in action? How can you get ready to spend time with Him?

8. What is the *one thing* you need to choose (Luke 10:42)?

_____

_____

ACT II

Location: Tomb
Time: Months Prior to Jesus' Death
Cast: _____
Title: _____

9. Read John 11:1–46 and then fill in the cast list and title for Act II.

Lazarus has been dead for four days. Mary and Martha grieve deeply. They both know Jesus is coming, but only Martha runs out to meet Him.

10. Jesus' response is unusual. What is the purpose of Lazarus' illness and resurrection (John 11:4, 41–42, 45)? How does this help explain why Jesus lingers an additional two days?

_____

_____

11. Why do you think John inserts verse 11:5? How sweet to be reminded that though tough times are ahead, Jesus loves his friends. What about us? Do we remember that Jesus loves us even when we are going through difficult times? Can you remember a time when you experienced his love in the midst of tragedy?

The disciples recognize that returning to Judea is dangerous and that it may even result in stoning. Jesus knows that it doesn't matter what danger exists; if He's walking in the light of His Father, He will not stumble. "A man who walks by day will not stumble, for he sees by this world's light. It is when he walks by night that he stumbles, for he has no light" (verses 9–10).

In verse 14, when Jesus explains Lazarus' condition to the disciples, no news has arrived about Lazarus. Jesus doesn't need to be told, because He already knows and because Lazarus is all part of a divine plan. The time is now perfect for Jesus to return to Mary, Martha, and Lazarus and reveal the greater good.

12. Mary and Martha react differently to the news that Jesus is finally arriving four days after Lazarus' death (verses 20–21, 30, 32–33). What do both Mary and Martha call Jesus (verses 21, 32)? Return to your Venn diagram and note the differences and similarities.

_____

_____

13. Martha makes a strong claim in verse 21. If her Lord had been there, what would *not* have happened? In verse 22, she goes even further. What is she asking for?

_____

_____

Though Martha understands her brother is a believer and will one day rise again, Jesus uses the opportunity to compare Lazarus with Himself and claims, "I am the Resurrection and the Life" (verses 25–26). We may have previously questioned some of Martha's attitudes and reactions, but just look at how she responds in verse 27.

14. Write her claim in verse 27 below.
"I believe…."

_____

_____

What about *you*, can you claim that Jesus is the Christ, the Son of God who has come into the world to explain God?

15. What is Jesus' reaction in verses 33 and 35?

_____

_____

16. What two contrasting opinions do the observers have in verses 36 and 37?

_____

_____

Jesus commands the stone to be moved. Though practical Martha knows that Jesus is capable of overcoming any situation, predictably she is concerned about the stench. The crowd then hears Jesus gives thanks for God's answer to a prayer He must have already prayed regarding Lazarus (verse 41).

17. Once again, in verses 45–46, we have two contrasting reactions of the observers and one big *"but"* separating them.

It doesn't seem to matter what miraculous acts Jesus does, some still do not believe. Yancey writes, "Although faith may produce miracles, miracles do not necessarily produce faith."[9] Some skeptics watch Lazarus emerge, with his wrappings clinging to His body and a cloth binding His face. Jesus commands the observers to release him from His bonds. But some who witness this resurrection are in greater bondage than Lazarus. Jesus knows the hearts of those watching—the hearts of men bound by disbelief. They will not accept that the Man who just raised Lazarus from the dead is the promised Messiah.

> "Did I not tell you that if you believed, you would see the glory of God?" (verse 40)

P.S. Our scene should end here, but we need to have a tag or P.S. Something will now be occurring in another location, behind the backs of Lazarus, Mary, and Martha, but certainly not unknown to Jesus.

Though many believe in Jesus after seeing His power (John 11:45), some tattle to the Pharisees, who then call an emergency meeting. The Sanhedrin is concerned about this Man performing miraculous signs, saying, "If we let him go on like this, everyone will believe in him, and then the Romans will come and take away both our place and our nation" (verse 48).

Then high priest Caiaphas proclaims, "You know nothing at all! You do not realize that it is better for you that one man die for the people than that the whole nation perish" (verses 49–50). He suggests that it would be better for Jesus to die rather than have the whole nation suffer under the hands of the Romans because of Him. However, Caiaphas' proclamation is ironically prophetic: It is indeed better that one man, Jesus, die so that all might not perish but have eternal life. John states this almost as an aside; "He did not say this on his own, but as high priest that year he prophesied that Jesus would die for the Jewish nation, and not only for that nation but also for the scattered children of God, to bring them together and make them one" (verses 51–52).

Jesus' miracles place Him in the center of the radar screen. The chief priests and Pharisees are concerned about the trouble this "wanna-be" king could stir up; they worry that His "kingship" could result in Rome restricting Jewish rights. The orders are given: if anyone knows where Jesus is, they should report it so He can be arrested. With a death threat hanging over His head, Jesus' mobility is reduced (verses 53–54). This chilling postscript leads us straight into tomorrow's Act III and a partial resolution of our drama.

Jesus' Words in Action: But before *tomorrow*, what have you learned *today*? In both Christ's living and in His dying, Jesus brings life. Martha didn't always focus on Jesus, but Martha knew who Jesus was. Jesus claims that He is the resurrection and the life and that believers will never die. He concludes with, "Do you believe this?" How about you? "Do you believe this?" Who do you say He is? Can you claim He is the Christ, the Son of God, the Resurrection and the Life? How did Jesus bring life to your life? Can you share His life with those around you who are dying spiritually or emotionally?

Thursday: Act III

Mary Anoints Jesus

Time:	Six days prior to Passover
Setting:	Bethany
Scripture:	John 12:1–11 (Matthew 26:6–16; Mark 14:1–11)
Cast:	_____
Title:	Mary Anoints Jesus

The curtain comes down on Act II with Jesus being stalked by His enemies. Now we read the rest of the story. The setting is Bethany, a small, quiet village near the Mount of Olives (see map on p. 16). This strategic location just two miles outside of Jerusalem will become an important home base for Jesus during His final week on earth. Act III occurs six days before Passover. We're jumping way ahead to just before Jesus rides into Jerusalem on a donkey.

In AD 2000, a person takes off his hat to show respect when entering a home. In AD 30, a person takes off his sandals and washes his feet before entering.[10] And yet, not even a servant is *required* to wash another man's feet.[11] Jesus would go beyond what was even required of a servant.

1. Read John 12:1–11 and then fill in the cast list above.

_____

_____

2. What is the role of each of the characters, Mary, Martha, and Lazarus? Record differences in your Venn diagram.

_____

_____

3. What actions does Mary take (John 12:3)?

_____

_____

The pure nard was a costly perfume or anointing oil made from an East Indian plant. What Mary pours on Jesus' feet is worth about three hundred denarii, the equivalent of what a commoner could earn in a year. The fragrance fills the room. Mary wipes her hair across Jesus' feet.

> By that act, she laid down her glory and, in essence, stood naked before her Lord. For in that culture, no proper woman ever let her hair down in public. A woman's hair was her glory, her identity, her ultimate sign of femininity, an intimate gift meant only for her husband. But for Mary, nothing was too extravagant for Jesus; she was even willing to risk her reputation. Like a lover before her beloved, she made herself vulnerable and fragile, open for rejection or rebuke.[12]

4. Who is disgusted, and why is he angered (verses 5–6)?

_____

_____

5. John is privy to a little background information on Judas, which foreshadows Judas' greed. What does John reveal about Judas in John 12:6?

_____

6. In your *own words*, write what Jesus says about Mary's generous actions (verses 7–8).

_____

_____

The needs and pleas for help are unending. Some generous women get "battle fatigue" and feel so overwhelmed they can't face any more needs on the frontline. But time spent in lavishly anointing Jesus with love, praise, and thanks will never exhaust us. *We* need to take time to bless *Him*; this helps us to continue blessing *others*.

Mary has the opportunity to anoint Jesus while He is still alive. The anointing is symbolic of many things, including the sacrifice, and it foreshadows Jesus' burial. She understands Jesus' prophecy whereas Judas has no understanding of why Mary would "waste" her money. This scene, and thus the entire play, ends with the ominous prophecy that Jesus will not always be among them on earth, preparing us for Jesus' last week.

Jesus' Words in Action: If *your* life were a three-act play, could you see the kind of growth exhibited by Mary or Martha? Could you write a statement below claiming who you believe Jesus to be? Be a *Martha* and try it.

Mary sat at Jesus' feet and listened to Him teach, and Mary anointed His feet. How about you? Could you sit at Jesus' feet and spend time with Him? Could you pour out your talents and your wealth in *worthship* or worship of Jesus? Be a *Mary* and try it.

Friday: The Bent Woman and Salome's Question

Today we'll study two contrasting women. One is an unnamed woman doubled over in sickness, and the other is

Salome, the wife of a prominent fisherman and mother of two of Jesus' disciples.

Looking Jesus in the eye must be hard for some of the women Jesus encounters around AD 30. Maybe they are full of shame or unworthiness. The unnamed woman we'll walk beside today is badly stooped with illness. They meet while Jesus is teaching in the synagogue on the Sabbath. Doctor Luke is the only Gospel writer to record this event.

📖 Read Luke 13:10–17.

1. How long had the woman been sick (verse 11)?

_____

What caused her sickness (verses 11, 16)?

_____

What are the symptoms (verse 11)?

_____

2. How does Jesus heal her (verse 12)?

_____

_____

3. What is the woman's two-part response (verse 13)?

_____

_____

4. Do we know if this woman *asked* for healing? Do we know if she had any faith? What drew Jesus to her side (verse 12)?

_____

_____

5. The synagogue officials are furious over Jesus' work on the Sabbath. What's the officials' argument (verse 14)?

_____

_____

> When God makes our crooked ways straight, do we immediately stand up and give Him the glory?

6. Jesus thinks fast. I love His response. "Don't you lead a donkey to water?" (verse 15). And then He calls the woman by name. What is the significance of the title he bestows upon her?

Daughter of _____ (verse 16)

7. What are the reactions of the two groups (verse 17)?

_____

_____

Opponents:
Multitude:

Remember, you're a woman in the crowd. If you listened in just a bit longer, you'd hear Jesus ask a question and answer it with two similes, one of which features a woman kneading bread. Isn't that just like Jesus? There are other women in the audience, and everything He says is also for their benefit (verses 18–21).

Jesus' Words in Action: Jesus noticed people in pain and went out of His way to help them. The result of His loving touch was evident to those who traveled beside Him. What encourages you about this woman's encounter with Jesus? How are you encouraged by what you see Jesus doing in the lives of those around you? In what ways are we bent? How could our straightening become a great witness to others?

The next woman we'll walk with is a close follower of Jesus. Not only is she a believer; both her sons choose to leave their father's occupation and follow Jesus. Like most mothers, she wants the best for her children and for them to have good positions. Salome is a woman who not only *wants* it; she *asks* for it.

From Matthew 27:56, we know that Salome is most likely the mother of the sons of Zebedee. As the wife of a successful fisherman, Salome is wealthy. We know from Mark's account of James' and John's calling that their father was in a boat with hired servants. Zebedee must have been able to go on working without the help of his "thunderous" sons.

Now let's read Matthew 20:20–28 and meet Salome. Jesus is on His way to Jerusalem when He begins to reveal that He will be mocked, scourged, and crucified. At this point Salome comes up to Jesus, bows down, and asks a question.

8. Write down her question (verse 21).

"_____that one of these _____ _____ of _____ may sit at your _____ and the other at your _____ in your_____."

9. Is Salome's request honest? Is there anything wrong with it? Have you ever felt you asked the Lord for a selfish request? What were the circumstances, and what happened?

_____

_____

10. Jesus answers with a question. "Can you drink the cup I am going to drink?" Who is in the audience answering, "We can" (verse 22)?

_____

_____

11. The answer may not be the one the disciples actually want to hear. What does Jesus mean that they will "indeed drink from His cup"? And why *can't* they sit on His right or His left (verse 23)?

_____

_____

How might Salome have reacted? What if she had walked out of the room in embarrassment and encouraged her sons to leave the ministry? What would she have missed? What about you? When friends or family correct you, or even when your Lord corrects you, can you take the criticism and learn from it? Can you remember a time when you accepted criticism with humility and benefited from the experience?

Jesus uses her "selfish" question to re-teach one of His most important messages.

12. Put Matthew 20:26–28, the heart of Jesus' message, into your own words.

_____

_____

Although Salome is rebuked and challenged, she stands corrected, and in Mark 15:40, we learn that she is at the cross with Mary Magdalene and Mary mother of James and Joses. In Mark 16:1, Salome returns to the tomb to bring spices to anoint Jesus' body. She grows from correction and doesn't wilt under chastisement. Thus, she becomes one of the first to know that Jesus has

> "You will indeed drink from my cup, but to sit at my right or left is not for me to grant. These places belong to those for whom they have been prepared by my Father." (Matthew 20:23)
>
>

risen from the dead.

13. Ironically, as a postscript, where does John recline at Jesus' Last Supper (John 13:23)?

_____

_____

Jesus hinted that John would outlive the other disciples (John 21:21–25). Later, John was exiled to Patmos and was the last writer to complete his Gospel.

And what about James? Acts 12:1–2 reads, "It was about this time that King Herod arrested some who belonged to the church, intending to persecute them. He had James, the brother of John, put to death with the sword." These two brothers were probably the first and last disciples (with the exception of Judas) to die.

Jesus' Words in Action: Jesus called us to serve and gave us the perfect example of service. In what ways could you be more of a servant today? Who is in need of your help? Pray for guidance and look for ways to serve the least, and look for ways to be last. In a world which encourages everyone to be the best and first, this will be a challenge. But Jesus' way is not the world's way. Be radical like Him. Don't be conformed to the world, but be transformed into His likeness (see Romans 12:2).

Saturday: "And Can It Be That I Should Gain?"

Scripture: "Your attitude should be the same as that of Christ Jesus: Who, being in very nature God, did not consider equality with God something to be grasped, but made himself nothing, taking the very nature of a servant, being made in human likeness." (Philippians 2:5–7)

These verses from Philippians would have helped Salome. Jesus made Himself _nothing_. He left the right hand of God in heavenly places, to take on the nature of a servant. "And Can It Be That I Should Gain" also beautifully follows Salome's story. Both title and refrain are phrased as questions. How _amazing_ that Jesus would die for the ones who caused Him pain. How _amazing_ that He would make Himself _nothing_ to come to earth to serve others and then die a criminal's death.

Each verse tells a story. Verse one begins with the question,

"Why am I included in the benefits of Christ's death?" Verse two explains Jesus' humility; finally, verse three concludes that because of His death, we are no longer condemned, but stand clothed in righteousness. But the best part of this hymn is the chorus. Its jubilant tune expresses Charles Wesley's sincere realization of salvation by faith.

"And Can It Be That I Should Gain"

And can it be, that I should gain
An interest in the Saviour's blood?
Died He for me, who caused His pain
For me, who Him to death pursued?
Amazing love! how can it be
That Thou, my God, shouldst die for me?

He left His Father's throne above,
So free, so infinite His grace,
Emptied Himself of all but love,
And bled for Adam's helpless race:
'Tis mercy all, immense and free;
For, O my God, it found out me!

No condemnation now I dread;
Jesus, and all in Him, is mine!
Alive in Him, my living Head,
And clothed in righteousness divine,
Bold I approach the eternal throne,
And claim the crown, through Christ my own.

> A mazing love! How can it be That Thou, my God, shouldst die for me?
>
> Charles Wesley, "And Can It Be That I Should Gain?"

Note: the last two lines of the first stanza are often repeated after each stanza as a chorus.

Response: *God Almighty, How amazing that You would come to earth to die for me! Help me to empty myself of all but love and take on the role of a servant. May I long to stand alive in You and clothed in Your righteousness! Help me understand the depth of your amazing love!*

Sunday: "My Jesus, I Love Thee"

Scripture: "Though you have not seen him, you love him; and even though you do not see him now, you believe in him and are filled with an inexpressible and glorious joy, for you are receiving the goal of your faith, the salvation of your souls" (1 Peter 1:8–9).

The women we've studied this week have walked with Jesus, seen Him, believed Him, and are filled with incredible joy and love. Although we have never seen Him face to face, we are filled with joy, faith, and the knowledge that we are saved. One day, we will meet Him face to face!

Has there been a time when you sang out with conviction, "If ever I loved Thee, my Jesus, 'tis now"? The women whose lives Jesus touched could have sung this hymn, and the women standing beneath the cross experienced the lyrics.

The words to this hymn may have been written by sixteen-year-old William Ralph Featherstone when he accepted Jesus. The song is fitting for Easter because it reminds us that Jesus is our gracious Redeemer and Savior, that He purchased our pardon on Calvary, wore a crown of thorns on His brow, and that one day we will wear a glittery crown when we adore Him in heaven so bright! *Oh My Jesus, I love Thee!*

> **I**f ever I loved Thee, my Jesus, 'tis now.
>
> William Featherstone, "My Jesus I Love Thee"

"My Jesus, I Love Thee"

My Jesus, I love Thee, I know Thou art mine
For Thee all the follies of sin I resign;
My gracious Redeemer, my Savior art Thou:
If ever I loved Thee, my Jesus, 'tis now.

I love Thee because Thou hast first loved me
And purchased my pardon on Calvary's tree;
I love Thee for wearing the thorns on Thy brow:
If ever I loved Thee, my Jesus, 'tis now.

In mansions of glory and endless delight
I'll ever adore Thee in heaven so bright;
I'll sing with the glittering crown on my brow,
"If ever I loved Thee, my Jesus, 'tis now."

Response: *My Jesus I love Thee. I know You are my Redeemer and my Savior. Thank you for first loving me and for paying the price for my sins on Calvary. I look forward to the day when I will meet You in heaven. Until then, may I love You more and more each day. Today, from the heart I pray, "If ever I loved You, Jesus, it's right now."*

Works Cited

1. Richards, Sue and Larry, *Every Woman in the Bible* (Nashville, TN: Thomas Nelson, 1999), 109.

2. Ray Vander Laan and Focus on the Family Video Series, *"That the World May Know: Faith Lessons on the Life and Ministry of the Messiah: The Rabbi"* (Grand Rapids, MI: Zondervan, 1996, 1998), Volume 3, Video 2.

3. *The MacArthur Study Bible*, (Nashville, TN: Thomas Nelson, Word Publishing, 1997), 1414.

4. Yancey, Philip, *The Jesus I Never Knew* (Grand Rapids, MI: Zondervan, 1995), 159.

5. *Matthew Henry Commentary*, in Accordance Bible software. CD-ROM, version 5.7. Oak Tree Software, Inc.

6. *The Ryrie Study Bible*, (Chicago, Illinois: Moody Press, 1976, 1978), 1472.

7. Richards, 158.

8. Ibid.

9. Yancey, 171.

10. Knight, George W., with Rayburn W. Ray, *The Illustrated Everyday Bible Companion: An All-in-One Resource for Everyday Bible Study* (Uhrichsville, OH: Barbour Publishing, Inc., 2005), 124.

11. Weaver, Joanna, *Having a Mary Heart in a Martha World: Finding Intimacy with God in the Busyness of Life* (Colorado Springs, CO: WaterBrook Press, 2000), 82.

12. Ibid., 171.

WEEK FOUR: JESUS ENTERS JERUSALEM

An Overview of the Last Week

Monday: Mark's Mission

In the first three weeks we've watched Jesus preach, teach, heal, and love, and we've known something was coming. His followers also knew Jesus was on enemy turf, but they couldn't fully comprehend what would happen to the man they wanted to be King.

This week marks the halfway point of our journey and is probably the most important because it's literally central to the rest of the study. You will skim-read the Gospel accounts of four writers to appreciate the events of Jesus' final week. As you read, look for something new or unfamiliar. The purpose of this week's study is to see the overview. Next week we'll zoom in for a closer look at Christ's teachings.

On Monday and Tuesday we'll cover Mark and Matthew and then break on Wednesday to look at maps of Jerusalem, timelines, and the major players. On Thursday and Friday we'll return to study Luke and John.

Each Gospel was written for a particular audience and thus with a specific and unique emphasis. Each writer had a different background. Matthew was a Jewish tax collector writing for the Jews. He emphasized Jesus as Messiah and the fulfillment of Old Testament prophecy. Missionary Mark focused almost half of his book on the last week of Jesus' life. Luke is a doctor with an eye for detail. Matthew, Mark, and Luke are known as the *Synoptic Gospels* because of their similarity. They provide a synopsis of His life from start to finish. John's Gospel differs greatly as you will soon find out!

Refer to this chart to help you understand differences in audience, occupation, and emphasis.

We'll begin with Mark, the shortest Gospel. John Mark, a fellow missionary friend of Paul and Barnabus, is the author. Whereas Matthew included a genealogy and much prophecy,

Text	Audience	Occupation	Emphasis
Matthew	Jews	Tax collector	Jesus is Messiah
Mark	Romans and Gentiles	Missionary	Jesus as Servant and Savior
Luke	Gentiles	Doctor	Jesus is Son of Man
John	All	Fisherman	Jesus is Son of God

Mark omitted these for his Gentile readers. But he did interpret certain Aramaic words (Mark 3:17; 5:41; 7:34; 15:22) for Romans, who might not have been familiar with them. He also used Latin on occasion instead of Greek (Mark 4:21; 6:26, 42; 15:15, 16, 39).[1] In the Book of Mark, everything happens quickly and immediately, moving the reader towards Christ's death and resurrection.

📖 Skim-read Mark 11—16 as if you don't know "the rest of the story." Place yourself in the audience. What is new or unfamiliar? Report your findings in the Mark column on page 92.

Tuesday: Matthew's Account

The fact that the New Testament begins with the Gospel of Matthew is significant because Matthew's Gospel connects Old Testament prophecy with New Testament fulfillment.[2] With almost 130 Old Testament references, Matthew quotes from the Old Testament more than the other Gospel writers. Because Matthew is writing to the Jews, he emphasizes Jesus as the Messiah they have long awaited. Watch for his frequent phrase, "that what was spoken through the prophet might be fulfilled."[3] Before becoming a disciple, Matthew collected taxes in Capernaum. He is the only one to cover the magi's visit, Mary's, Joseph's, and Jesus' escape to Egypt, and the Sermon on the Mount.[4]

📖 Skim-read Matthew 21—28, and imagine yourself as one of Jesus' followers ascending the long, dusty road to Jerusalem.

Wednesday: Jerusalem Overview

WANTED: YESHU HANNOZRI
He shall be stoned because he has practiced sorcery and enticed Israel to apostasy. Anyone who can say anything in his favor, let him come forward and plead on his behalf. Anyone who knows where he is, let him declare it to the Great Sanhedrin in Jerusalem.[5]

During Passover in AD 30, Jerusalem's population has swelled from fifty thousand residents to perhaps a quarter of a million or even two to three million.[6] The crowded city spills over into tents outside the walls. The Jewish pilgrims cannot understand that this would be the most significant Passover in history. This Passover would end all need for future Passovers. Once this Passover lamb is crucified, His blood would cover all sins for every person forever.

Today we'll look at the geography of the city and its people. As you read, underline key words, points, or characters that are unfamiliar, or make notes in the margins so you can return to these pages as reference material for the final weeks of our journey.

Geography: Map of New Testament Jerusalem

Jerusalem, a three-hundred acre city with a circumference of three miles, is centrally situated between the Mediterranean and Dead seas in the dry hill country. This intersection marks a central point for trade routes. At various times, Persians, Greeks, and Romans occupied Jerusalem's walled city. In 37 BC, King Herod had Jewish workers construct strong walls, a fortress, a moat, the Herodium, and aqueducts. The architecture *was* phenomenal; we say *was* because the city of Jerusalem was eventually destroyed in AD 70 just as Jesus had prophesied.

Looking at the map on the next page, you'll see King Herod's Palace and the Kidron Valley (at the foot of the Mount of Olives/Offense where the Garden of Gethsemane exists). Looking at the map, within the city walls you will find Golgotha, and the Praetorium. Jesus did not remain in the city each evening; more likely He stayed in Mary and Martha's home in nearby Bethany or in the Garden of Gethsemane.

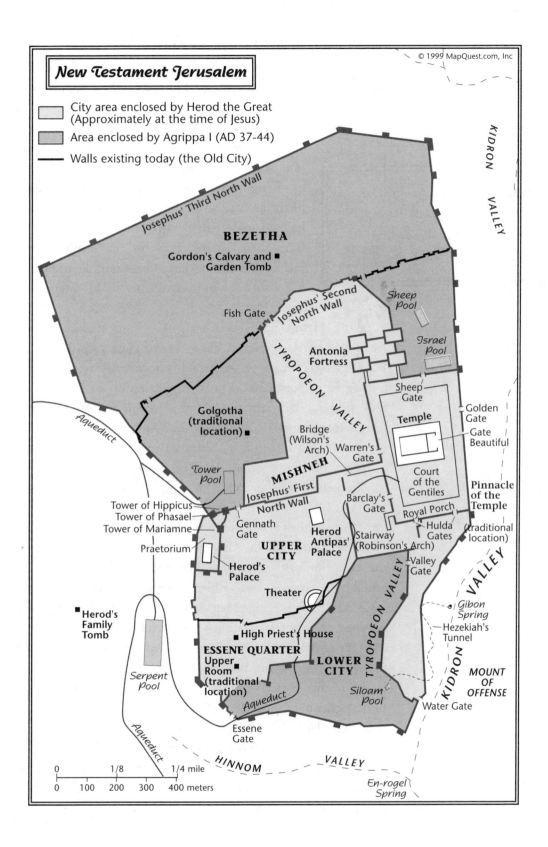

New Testament Jerusalem

© 1999 MapQuest.com, Inc

City area enclosed by Herod the Great
(Approximately at the time of Jesus)

Area enclosed by Agrippa I (AD 37-44)

Walls existing today (the Old City)

KIDRON VALLEY

Josephus' Third North Wall

BEZETHA

Gordon's Calvary and ■
Garden Tomb

Sheep Pool

Fish Gate

Josephus' Second North Wall

Israel Pool

TYROPOEON VALLEY

Antonia Fortress

Sheep Gate

Golden Gate

Golgotha
(traditional
location) ■

Temple

Gate Beautiful

Bridge
(Wilson's
Arch)

Warren's
Gate

Tower Pool

MISHNEH

Court
of the
Gentiles

Pinnacle
of the
Temple

Josephus' First
North Wall

Barclay's
Gate

Royal Porch

Tower of Hippicus
Tower of Phasael
Tower of Mariamne

Gennath
Gate

Herod
Antipas'
Palace

Stairway
(Robinson's Arch)

Hulda
Gates

(traditional
location)

Praetorium

UPPER
CITY

Valley
Gate

Herod's
Palace

Theater

TYROPOEON VALLEY

VALLEY

Herod's
Family
Tomb

Gibon
Spring

Hezekiah's
Tunnel

■ High Priest's House

ESSENE QUARTER

LOWER
CITY

KIDRON

MOUNT
OF
OFFENSE

Serpent
Pool

Upper
Room
(traditional
location)

Aqueduct

Siloam
Pool

Water Gate

Aqueduct

Essene
Gate

HINNOM   VALLEY

Aqueduct

| 0 | 1/8 | 1/4 mile |

| 0 | 100 | 200 | 300 | 400 meters |

En-rogel
Spring

Major Political and Religious Leaders:

The major political and religious players are all men. Though they may be difficult to relate to, remember: these are real people with names and personalities and hopes and dreams. How do they affect the lives of women in Jerusalem at that time?

The one woman on the list (Pilate's wife) is the lone voice of reason.

King Herod the Great was king at Jesus' birth. He was so frightened by the baby that he had all male babies two years and younger in Bethlehem slain. Herod's accomplishments include rebuilding Jerusalem's temple and creating a port city in Caesarea on the Mediterranean Sea.

> "Foxes have holes and birds of the air have nests, but the Son of Man has no place to lay his head." (Matthew 8:20)

King Herod had many sons. His sons include Herod Antipas, Archelaus, Herod Philip I, and Herod Phillip II.[7] At King Herod's death in 4 BC, his territories were divided among his descendents. The next generation of Herods was also ruthless. (In Matthew 2:22–23, Joseph and Mary do not return from Egypt to Judea because Archelaus is ruler. They choose instead to settle in Nazareth in Galilee, fulfilling the prophecy that Jesus would be a Nazarene).

Archelaus is the son who ruled Samaria, Judaea, and Idumaea (4 BC–AD 6). Because of his inability to govern, he lost his authority to an appointed prefect or procurator. Procurator Pontius Pilate later assumed Archelaus' region with the exception of the area of Galilee and Perea, which was governed by Archelaus' *brother* Herod Antipas.[8] Can you see why Jesus is later ping-ponged back and forth from Pilate to Herod Antipas? Whose responsibility is Jesus anyway?

Herod Antipas is the son who ruled Galilee and Perea and had John the Baptist beheaded. Jesus called him "that fox" (Luke 13:32). Herod Antipas interrogated Jesus, hoping to see Him perform a miracle or two, and then ridiculed Him (Matthew 14:1–10; Mark 6:14–28; Luke 3:1, 19, 20; 13:31; 23:7–12). He was a political enemy of Pilate until uniting against Jesus. "That day Herod and Pilate became friends— before this they had been enemies" (Luke 23:12).[9] Herod Antipas was later deposed.

Herod Agrippa I is the grandson of Herod the Great and ruled from AD 37–44 over the large region of Palestine, which included Samaria and Judea. He persecuted members of the early Church, imprisoned Peter, and killed James. His death, like his grandfather's, was ugly (Acts 12:21–23).

Annas was the "former" high priest (AD 7–14). His daughter married Caiaphas, who assumed or shared leadership with Annas as president of the Sanhedrin. The Roman procurator deposed him.

Caiaphas served as high priest from AD 27–36 and was Annas' son-in-law and successor to the high priest. Caiaphas, along with the Sanhedrin, voted to have Jesus killed, though Caiaphas tried to pass off responsibility to the Governor of Rome. He is most remembered for his prophetic comment in which he says it would be better "that one man die for the people than that the whole nation perish" (John 11:49–52).

Pontius Pilate was the sixth Roman procurator and believed in many gods.[10] He served from AD 26–36 as Jerusalem's governor and Rome's representative from afar. The governor usually stayed in Caesarea and preferred Rome for its theatre and excitement. But he came to Jerusalem during times of trouble, an uprising, or when great crowds gathered, such as during Passover. Pilate hated the Jews and had little regard for their religious practices. "Now there were some present at that time who told Jesus about the Galileans whose blood Pilate had mixed with their sacrifices" (Luke 13:1). Because of his ignorance of their religious practices, he made grievous and sometimes idolatrous errors and earned their disrespect, which lessened his authority.

Pilate's wife had more sense (or was scared "senseless" by a dream) and tried to warn him of the danger of convicting an innocent man. Pontius Pilate's famous line is, "What is truth?" Though the *Way* the *Truth* and the *Life* stood before him, he didn't recognize Him. After Pilate falsely slaughtered hundreds of Samaritans near Gerizim, his political career dissolved.[11]

Jews had some legal status and religious freedom, but they were persecuted for their faith. They were set apart because they didn't believe in the Greek and Roman gods; they practiced unusual religious customs, didn't work on the Sabbath, held no political positions, and avoided certain foods.

Beginning in roughly 145 BC, the Jews divided into groups including the Essenes, Pharisees, and Sadducees. These factions believed in various degrees of political separation. Studying their motivations will help you understand their animosity toward Jesus. Some believed in collaboration with Rome while others wanted separation.

Many of the groups listed are clearly collaborationists or separationists. The Pharisees wanted both to be separate and to collaborate. They were principled but practical. They legalistically followed their Jewish rules but because of past persecution, picked which battles to fight.[12] Understanding their fears and desires will help you see why they would have the Son of God killed. The descriptions below begin with those who desired separation the most and end with the staunchest advocates for collaboration.

Political Continuum

Separationists   Collaborationists

Essenes Zealots Pharisees Sanhedrin Sadducees

The Essenes were a mystical pacifist sect formed around 100 BC. As separationists they withdrew and lived in desert caves like monks, committing themselves to purity. While awaiting the Messiah, they lived strict lives with ritual baths, a strict diet, no defecating on the Sabbath, sharing their goods, and wearing no jewelry.[13]

Zealots were separationists who rebelled against Roman authority because they believed only God could be king. Unlike the peaceful Essenes, they believed in physically rebelling against authority. They later became lawless, using a sica or Roman dagger to assault their victims and thereby earning the name *Sicarri*.

Pharisees were both separationists and collaborationists. Pharisee literally means, "to separate."[14] For the most part they wanted to be separate from Roman government, but occcasionally they sided with the Sanhedrin in collaboration efforts with Rome. Although they monitored every letter of the law regarding purity and Sabbath practices, they only gave *lip,* not *heart,* service to their beliefs. They were self-righteous, judgmental, and proud. Jesus repeatedly chastised them, "You hypocrites! Isaiah was right when he prophesied about you: 'These people honor me with their lips, but their hearts are far from me. They worship me in vain; their teachings are but rules taught by men'" (Matthew 15:7–9). With 613 commands (365 of which are prohibitions) they had a lot of work keeping up with the rules![15]

The Sanhedrin was a longstanding group of seventy-one members made up of twenty-four chief priests and forty-six elders including scribes, primarily made up of Sadducees.[16] This could be compared to a Jewish supreme court, with the chief justice voting and ruling as high priest. The Sanhedrin members were collaborationists who wanted to keep everyone in line. Rome allowed them a degree of power, and they gave Rome peace in return. They tried to silence the Jews so there would be no insurrection or revolt. The Sanhedrin was fashioned after Moses' Council in Numbers 11:16[17] and formed near the time of the Maccabees.

The **Chief Priests** were Sadducees who represented the Jews, offered animal sacrifices and prayers, and were examples of the ultimate High Priest to come. They took turns ministering in Jerusalem and had great religious responsibility. Because their power was sometimes purchased, their roles became highly political.

Priests numbered approximately seven thousand at the time of Christ. There were also temple guards and rabbis.[18]

Scribes were the lawyers or secretaries of states, and they were usually Pharisees who taught the oral and written laws in public places.[19]

Elders were men of political, religious, and social authority and influence.

The Sadducees were rich and powerful and loved the profit gained from the temple tax.[20] They did not believe in divine intervention or an afterlife and so they lived their life on earth without fear of consequences or with the goal of rewards. Jesus called them "hypocrites" and a "wicked and adulterous gener-ation" (Matthew 16:1–4; 22:23). They were deists and skeptics who aligned themselves with Romans and King Herod. They did not want to lose their status and worldly comforts. In our continuum they were obviously collaborationists who didn't want anything to alter their current situation.[21]

Herodians were political Jews who followed Herod.

Jerusalem, Spring of AD 30 Timeline of Events
Scholars differ on the exact dates of some of these events, but this overview should give you an idea of the *order*. The major difference many scholars have is whether Jesus was crucified on Thursday versus Friday. There are strong reasons presented for either day. Let this thought intrigue *you* to research further.

Sunday	Monday	Tuesday	Wednesday	Thursday	Friday	Saturday
Jesus enters Jerusalem	Jesus curses fig tree	Jesus ques-tioned by Sanhedrin, Pharisees and Sadducees	Judas meets with religious leaders	Disciples pre-pare for Passover	Trials: Annas and Caiaphas	Soldiers secure the tomb
	Jesus cleanses the Temple			Jesus washes disciples' feet	Trial: Pilate	
		Jesus teaches parables and prophesies		Jesus betrayed by Judas	Trial: Herod	
					Trial: Pilate	
		Anointed by Mary (some believe in this date; others believe it to be previous Saturday)		Passover and Lord's Supper	Jesus walks to Golgotha	
				Jesus prays in the garden	Jesus hung on the cross	
				Jesus arrested	Jesus buried in Joseph's tomb	

Thursday: Luke's Diagnosis

Now that you've had the Wednesday break, you're ready for the longest Gospel account! Though you've read two fairly similar gospels, almost half of Luke's Gospel is unique.[22] In addition to his Gospel, Luke also is the author of the book of Acts.

Physician Luke presents Jesus as the *Son of Man* to his Gentile audience. His presentation reveals a sympathetic, compassionate Savior. Luke is the one most likely to write about women[23] and often pairs men and women in his stories, giving the women the more favorable depiction.[24]

Skim-read Luke 19:28—Luke 24. Note Dr. Luke's attention to detail. Perhaps the doctor in him makes him so observant. As you read, watch for details that you may not have observed in the other three Gospels. What is Jesus revealing that is new to you? Record this in the Luke column on page 92.

Friday: John's Record

If Passover week is now feeling familiar, that's good. If it seems *too* familiar, that's okay because John's Gospel will give you a whole new perspective.

The Gospel was written by John, who was the brother of James and one of the sons of Zebedee and Salome. John was a wealthy Jew, a fisherman called by Christ a "son of thunder" (Mark 3:17), and he was recognized as the "disciple whom Jesus loved" (John 21:20, 24). John focuses on many of Jesus' final teachings and emphasizes salvation and eternal life. His writings highlight that since the beginning, God and Jesus were One. Jesus was here long before AD or BC, before all time. The book of John records the seven "I am" claims we studied in Week One, but it specifically focuses on only seven of Jesus' miracles.[25]

Skim-read John 12:12—John 21. Place yourself as a Passover pilgrim waving the palm branch high as Jesus enters the city. Look at His lessons at Passover and in the garden. What is Jesus teaching you today?

_____

_____

Saturday: "Alas! and Did My Savior Bleed?"

Scripture: "It was now about the sixth hour, and darkness came over the whole land until the ninth hour." (Luke 23:44)

We've been reading about Jesus' final week on earth and how terribly He was mistreated. His torturous persecution begs the question, "Why did He die for such an ungrateful mob?" Isaac Watts wrote, "Alas! And did my Savior Bleed?" a hymn that asks, "Why would Jesus die for someone such as me?"

The questioner realizes he can never repay Jesus for His sacrifice, but He does devote his life to thankfulness and complete commitment to his Lord.

Isaac Watts authored the text. Watts also wrote "Joy to the World!"—but the song was not meant to be a Christmas carol; it celebrates the *Second* Coming of Christ. Watts had been frustrated by dreary hymns until his father challenged him to write hymns of joy. Watts penned six hundred hymns in his lifetime.

"Alas! and Did My Savior Bleed?"

Alas! and did my Savior bleed and did my Sovereign die?
Would he devote that sacred head for such a one as I?

Was it for sins that I had done—he groaned upon the tree?
Amazing pity! Grace unknown! And love beyond degree!

Well might the sun in darkness hide and shut his glories in,
When Christ, the mighty Maker, died, for man, the creature's sin.

Thus might I hide my shamed face while his dear Cross appears,
Dissolve my heart in thankfulness, and melt mine eyes to tears.

But drops of grief can ne'er repay the debt of love I owe:
Here, Lord, I give myself to thee; 'Tis all that I can do.

Refrain
At the cross, at the cross where I first saw the light,
And the burden of my heart rolled away,
It was there by faith I received my sight,
And now I am happy all the day!

This decidedly Easter hymn encourages deeply personal soul searching for the singer facing the Lenten season.

Response: *Jesus, Your love is beyond degree. My heart is thankful. I want to be completely committed to You. Help me devote myself to Your service, O Lord.*

Would he devote that sacred head for such a one as I?

"Alas! and Did My Savior Bleed?"
Isaac Watts

Sunday: "Beneath the Cross of Jesus"

Scripture: "If anyone would come after me, he must deny himself and take up his cross daily and follow me" (Luke 9:23).

Like Fanny Crosby, Elizabeth Clephane was limited by illness and also wrote about being beneath the cross. She wrote but eight hymns before she died at age 39. "Beneath the Cross of Jesus" was written in 1868, the summer before her death, but it was published posthumously. Elizabeth Clephane was a woman who bore not only the cross of illness, but also the fruit of praise.

Laden with Bible verses, a studious listener could match the hymn's many references with the following hidden treasures of Scripture: Isaiah 32:2, Psalm 63:1, Jeremiah 9:2, Isaiah 28:12, Isaiah 4:6, and Matthew 11:28–30.

> I take, O cross, thy shadow for my abiding place—
>
> "Beneath the Cross of Jesus," Elizabeth Clephane

Can you picture this song being sung by the Samaritan woman, or the adulterous woman, or the bent woman? They would understand the Jesus depicted in this hymn.

"Beneath the Cross of Jesus"

Beneath the cross of Jesus I fain would take my stand
The shadow of a mighty rock within a weary land;
A home within the wilderness, a rest upon the way
From the burning of the noon day heat and the burden of the day.

Upon that cross of Jesus mine eye at times can see
The very dying form of One who suffered there for me;
And from my smitten heart with tears two wonders I confess—
The wonders of His glorious love and my own worthlessness.

I take, O cross, thy shadow for my abiding place—
I ask no other sunshine than the sunshine of His face;
Content to let the world go by, to know no gain nor loss,
My sinful self my only shame, my glory all the cross.

Response: *Thank you, Lord, for your glorious love revealed through your suffering on the cross. I humbly bow at the cross, acknowledge my sin, and accept your forgiveness. Help me reach out to others with that same sacrificial and generous love.*

Reading the Passion of Christ

Jot down what is new or less familiar to you from each Gospel.

Matthew 21—28	Mark 11—16
Luke 19:28—24	John 12:12—John 21

Works Cited

1. *Nelson's Complete Book of Bible Maps and Charts* (Nashville, TN: Thomas Nelson, 1996), 327.

2. Ibid., 311.

3. Ibid., 313.

4. Ibid.

5. Maier, Paul L., *In the Fullness of Time: A Historian Looks at Christmas, Easter, and the Early Church* (Grand Rapids, MI: Kregel, 1991), 114.

6. MacArthur, John, *The Murder of Jesus: A Study of How Jesus Died* (Nashville, TN: Thomas Nelson, 2000), 15.

7. *Nelson's Complete Book of Bible Maps and Charts*, 309–310.

8. Gower, Ralph, *The New Manners and Customs of Bible Times* (Chicago: Moody Press, 1987), 278–280.

9. MacArthur, 177.

10. Ibid., 184.

11. Ibid., 174.

12. Yancey, Philip, *The Jesus I Never Knew* (Grand Rapids, MI: Zondervan, 1995), 63.

13. Ibid., 61.

14. *Easton's Bible Dictionary* in Accordance Bible software. CD-ROM, version 5.7. Oak Tree Software, Inc.

15. J. Hampton Keathley, III, Th.M, "The Contention Among the Pharisees," http://www.bible.org.

16. MacArthur, 103. *The MacArthur Study Bible* (Nashville, TN:

Thomas Nelson, Word Publishing, 1997), 1488.

17. MacArthur, 103.

18. Bishop, Jim, *The Day Christ Died: The Inspiring Classic on the Last 24 Hours of Jesus' Life* (San Francisco: Harper, 1957), 40.

19. Ibid., 39.

20. *The MacArthur Study Bible* (Nashville, TN: Thomas Nelson, Word Publishing, 1997), 1488.

21. *Easton's Bible Dictionary* in Accordance Bible software. CD-ROM, version 5.7. Oak Tree Software, Inc. Yancey, 62.

22. *Nelson's Complete Book of Bible Maps and Charts,* 336.

23. Ibid., 336.

24. Richards, Sue and Larry, *Every Woman in the Bible* (Nashville, TN: Thomas Nelson, 1999), 163–168.

25. *Nelson's Complete Book of Bible Maps and Charts,* 347.

Increasing Tension

Last week we looked at Jesus' final week in Jerusalem from four viewpoints. Now we'll focus on specific events that occurred at the beginning of that week.

On Sunday, Jesus rides into Jerusalem. To see Him enter with accolades must be thrilling to onlookers. But to see public reaction to Jesus change course so drastically must be devastating to His followers.

As a musician, I notice how the score affects a movie. If I were director of a film about Christ, my background music for the Passion Week would be somber with an intensifying drumbeat. The major key would quickly change to a minor and include great harmonic dissonance to underscore a horrible anticipation.

Monday: A Political Entry into Jerusalem

Jesus and His followers come from Jericho (over 800 feet below sea level) climbing to Jerusalem (2500 feet above sea level).[1] It's a twisting, dusty path ascending over three thousand feet in twenty miles through a barren and rocky landscape filled with steep ledges.[2] This wilderness area was the setting for the parable of the Good Samaritan and Jesus' forty days of temptation. These "Judean badlands" are crowded with pilgrims arriving for Passover.[3]

The Sunday prior to Passover is lamb selection day, the day each family chooses a perfect lamb for the Passover sacrifice. God's timing is deliberate. Jesus enters Jerusalem with the chosen Passover lambs because He *is* the Perfect Lamb chosen by God.[4]

📖 Read Luke 19:28–34.

Passover is a celebration commemorating the Israelites' liberation from Egyptian bondage. From time to time, radical Jewish insurgents would emerge during these celebrations claiming to be the Messiah, which caused outbreaks and the slaughter of many by the Romans. Crowd-control incidents like these necessitated increased numbers of Roman soldiers.[5]

1. Look at Luke 19:37–38. What happens as they near the place where the road descends? Why might they have previously been quiet?

_____

_____

What about the women who are part of this crowd? What do they see? Does a military victory matter to a group of women who have been delivered by His love and freed from limiting rules and demons? Are the women remembering what happened the last time Jesus came to Jerusalem?

The previous winter (circa AD 29), after being warned by the Pharisees to leave because Herod wanted to kill Him, Jesus replied,

> Go tell that fox, "I will drive out demons and heal people today and tomorrow, and on the third day I will reach my goal." In any case, I must keep going today and tomorrow and the next day—for surely no prophet can die outside Jerusalem! (Luke 13:32–33)

And after that outburst, Jesus' words became sorrowful. He used nurturing, feminine, and motherly terms to show how deeply He cared for Jerusalem.

> O Jerusalem, Jerusalem, you who kill the prophets and stone those sent to you, how often I have longed to gather your children together, as a hen gathers her chicks under her wings, but you were not willing! Look, your house is left to you desolate. I tell you, you will not see me again until you say, 'Blessed is he who comes in the name of the Lord.' (Luke 13:34–35)

This is the moment Jesus foretold. Now the followers shout the very words of Old Testament scripture Jesus had prophesied.

2. Underline the prophecy from Psalms 118:25–27 below. Remember "Hosanna!" means "Save us!"

> O LORD, save us; O LORD, grant us success.
> Blessed is he who comes in the name of the LORD.

From the house of the LORD we bless you.

The LORD is God, and he has made his light shine upon us.

With boughs in hand, join in the festal procession up to the horns of the altar.

3. What do you know about the colt Jesus rides (Luke 19:30)?

_____

Who would tell someone to untie a stranger's colt with the excuse, "The Lord needs it?" (Luke 19:31). Who would choose a colt that had *never been ridden*? Why, someone who is Lord of all![6] And why an *unbroken* colt? A colt that had never been sat upon was considered more holy (Numbers 19:2; Deuteronomy 21:3; 1 Samuel 6:7)[7] and true to Matthew's recording of prophecy; he points out that this is what the prophets foretold (Matthew 21:3–5).

> "Rejoice greatly, O Daughter of Zion! Shout, Daughter of Jerusalem! See, your king comes to you, righteous and having salvation, gentle and riding on a donkey, on a colt, the foal of a donkey." (Zechariah 9:9)
>
>

Read Luke 19:35–40.

The people throw their cloaks on the colt as well as the roads—symbolic of the arrival of a military leader. In 2 Kings 9:13, the entry of King Jehu was heralded with cloaks spread beneath him. With Jesus, the crowd acknowledges their hope in a military hero.[8]

Mark and Matthew's accounts add that branches cut in the fields and from the trees are spread on the road (Matthew 21:8; Mark 11:7–8).

Greeks and Romans dubbed Palestine as the land of palms because of the many forty-to-eighty foot trees flourishing in the region. Their feathery fronds fanned out almost 6–12 feet in praise. Even Revelation 7:9 prophesies the use of palms when we greet the Lamb: ". . . from every nation, tribe, people and language, standing before the throne and in front of the Lamb. They were wearing white robes and were holding palm branches in their hands."[9]

> "They hurried and took their cloaks and spread them under him on the bare steps. Then they blew the trumpet and shouted, 'Jehu is king!' " (2 Kings 9:13)
>
>

The palm branch at this time is a national symbol for freedom. It was the symbol on a previous Jewish coin used in the Macabbean time of freedom and is a symbol for the zealot freedom fighters. Waving a palm branch means, "We will be victorious!" It is similar to waving a national flag and cheering for your country. Those hailing Him as King are looking for peace with the wrong battle plan and with politically charged words.[10] This is not the kind of victory the Lamb of God and Prince of Peace had in mind.[11]

Whenever I've played a character in our local passion play, Jesus' entrance has been triumphant. I feel the joy and exuberance of hailing Him and waving my palm branch. Children weave themselves between the adults, calling out, "Jesus is coming! Jesus is coming!"

Two thousand years later, on Palm Sunday, we sing "All Glory Laud and Honor," which shows the contrast of the children's *sweet* hosannas and the adults' longing for a King.

> *All glory, laud, and honor—to thee, Redeemer, King!*
> *To whom the lips of children made sweet hosannas ring.*
> *Thou art the King of Israel, thou David's royal Son,*
> *Who in the Lord's Name comest, the King and Blessed One.*

The song recognizes that Jesus is indeed the *King of Israel*, the *Blessed One*. The people of Jesus' day understood that. But they assumed Jesus was a King coming in *might*—a King who would deliver *politically*. However, Jesus came to deliver *spiritually*. Although the lines for the script read:

"Hosanna!"

"Blessed is he who comes in the name of the Lord!" (Mark 11:9; John 12:13)

"Hosanna!" "Blessed is the coming kingdom of our father David!" (Mark 11:9–10)

"Blessed is the King of Israel!" (John 12:13)

"Hosanna to the Son of David!" "Hosanna in the highest!" (Matthew 21:9)

Their underlying meaning is "*SAVE US! SAVE US! We're sick of Rome! Deliver us! Give us freedom! SAVE US! SAVE US!*"[12]

Save us! Save us! That's just what Jesus longs to do, but from the inside out.

4. In what areas does Jesus want to change *you* from the inside out?

_____

_____

5. The mood changes. Who ends this joyful scene and why (Luke 19:39)?

_____

_____

The Jewish leaders want the people to quiet down. A crowd of people shouting "Save us from Rome!" jeopardizes the status quo. At this moment, how does Jesus deal with the passion of the people? Luke adds a most revealing detail: Jesus weeps.

📖 Read Luke 19:41–44.

Jesus cries twice in the Bible. He cried silently at Lazarus' death and now aloud for the death of Jerusalem.[13] Is it any wonder that Jesus cries? What disappointment and sorrow!

> *Oh Jerusalem, if you only knew what will come to you in AD 70 when Titus will set scaffolding and embankments around your marble and gold temple and set fire to it. The city packed with Passover pilgrims will starve under siege. Section by section you will fall, and thousands of men, women, and children will be dashed to the ground. The "lucky" survivors will become a part of the Roman circus.*[14]

His followers can't see that, but Jesus can. And He weeps.

6. Why do you suppose the women thought He was crying?

_____

_____

A man who can cry with compassion is a powerful draw. Here the *Prince of Peace* cries for Jerusalem, a name like *shalom*, the Hebrew word for *peace*. But Jerusalem is about to experience anything *but* peace.

Jesus must be further saddened by what he confronts at the temple. It's late and so He leaves and returns to Bethany, perhaps to the home of Lazarus, Mary, and Martha (Mark 11:11). He will cleanse the temple the next day when the Hosannas continue and incite the chief priests and teachers of the law. But Jesus' scripturally based response from the Old Testament reminds them that praise is ordained.

The blind and the lame came to him at the temple, and he healed them. But when the chief priests and the teachers of the law saw the wonderful things he did and the children shouting in the temple area, "Hosanna to the Son of David," they were indignant.

"Do you hear what these children are saying?" they asked him. "Yes," replied Jesus, "have you never read, 'From the lips of children and infants you have ordained praise'?" (Matthew 21:14–16)

Jesus' Words in Action: The most triumphant scene turns to tears. What would you have thought standing there amongst the crowd? When have you experienced a mountaintop experience only to find yourself in the valley of despair?

And what about his plea of longing to nurture? Do you let him draw you to Him like a mother hen gathers her chicks? Today, carry that picture with you. Let Him tuck you beneath His wings. "Keep me as the apple of your eye; hide me in the shadow of your wings" (Psalms 17:8). And what about the praise? Silence the foe and the avenger by lifting praise to the Lamb of God. Praise is ordained by God!

> "From the lips of children and infants you have ordained praise because of your enemies, to silence the foe and the avenger." (Psalm 8:2)

Tuesday: Just What Kind of King Did the People Expect?

As early as the third chapter of Genesis, God began revealing His plan of salvation. Matthew Henry comments on Genesis 3:15 that Christ's heel had been bruised, but not His head, and that Christ ultimately would triumph over Satan, delivering the crushing wound to the serpent's head.[15]

The salvation stories continue, and God made a covenant with His people. When God called Abraham to sacrifice his son on the altar, Abraham was willing, but God provided a ram instead. Because of Abraham's obedience, God made a covenant with Abraham that his descendants would be numerous, take possession of the cities, and all offspring would be blessed. The entire story

> "And I will put enmity between you and the woman, and between your offspring and hers; he will crush your head, and you will strike his heel." (Genesis 3:15)

prophesied God's deliverance through His only Son, Jesus (Genesis 22:16–18).

Similarly, the Lord warned Noah of a flood and instructed him to build an ark. Noah obeyed and was saved through faith.

The widow Ruth followed God and met her kinsman redeemer, Boaz. Boaz paid the price to purchase Ruth as His wife and became the great-grandfather of King David. God later promised this shepherd King that his offspring would be the ultimate Shepherd-King Messiah.

So the people knew that a Messiah would come. But His followers gravitated toward a kingly Messiah with power, glory, and authority. This Son of Man would sit at the right hand of God.[16]

> "He remembers his covenant forever, the word he commanded, for a thousand generations, the covenant he made with Abraham, the oath he swore to Isaac." (Psalm 105:8–9)

Max Lucado writes,

> To the Jew the Son of Man was a symbol of triumph. The conqueror. The equalizer. The score-settler. The big brother. The intimidator. The Starship Enterprise. The right arm of the High and Holy. The king who roared down from the heavens in a fiery chariot of vengeance and anger toward those who have oppressed God's holy people.[17]

The *Son of Man* represents power and glory. The *suffering servant* does not. Though Old Testament scriptures in Psalms and Isaiah also prophesied a grim death for a Suffering Servant, His followers in AD 30 aren't looking for a Lamb; they are looking for a triumphant King.

Jim Bishop adds in *The Day Christ Died*,

> In the Psalms, the Messiah is seen in prophecy coming as a king, crushing Israel's enemies, purging Jerusalem, routing nations. After that the Messiah was to govern Palestine in peace and justice, and the Gentiles would come from the ends of the earth to contemplate the glory of Jerusalem.[18]

What about the women? Do they long for that same sort of King? What do *they* want to be free from? Let's look back at the Old Testament and see what the men and women of AD 30 are looking and hoping for.

1. This first scripture passage is usually heard at Christmas but is far more applicable at Easter. Underline words that people longing for a redeemer may have clung to, hoped for, and focused on. Write your two favorite words below.

> For to us a child is born, to us a son is given, and the government will be on his shoulders. And he will be called Wonderful Counselor, Mighty God, Everlasting Father, Prince of Peace. Of the increase of his government and peace there will be no end. He will reign on David's throne and over his kingdom, establishing and upholding it with justice and righteousness from that time on and forever. The zeal of the LORD Almighty will accomplish this. (Isaiah 9:6–7)

"In the future you will see the Son of Man sitting at the right hand of the Mighty One and coming on the clouds of heaven." (Matthew 26:64)

2. Jesus is from Nazareth. The word "Nazareth" may come from the word *netzer* or *branch*. Jesus is a descendant or *shoot* from the stump of Jesse (David's father), a stump that bears much fruit. Is it any wonder that it was this passage in which Jesus announced that scripture had been fulfilled (Luke 4:16–30)? Continue to select and underline favorite words and then list below.

> A shoot will come up from the stump of Jesse; from his roots a Branch will bear fruit. The Spirit of the LORD will rest on him—the Spirit of wisdom and of understanding, the Spirit of counsel and of power, the Spirit of knowledge and of the fear of the LORD—and he will delight in the fear of the LORD. He will not judge by what he sees with his eyes, or decide by what he hears with his ears; but with righteousness he will judge the needy, with justice he will give decisions for the poor of the earth. He will strike the earth with the rod of his mouth; with the breath of his lips he will slay the wicked. Righteousness will be his belt and faithfulness the sash around his waist. The wolf will live with the lamb, the leopard will lie down with the goat, the calf and the lion and the yearling together; and a little child will lead them. (Isaiah 11:1–6)

3. Though Jesus was raised in Nazareth, He was born in Bethlehem. Out of that small village would come a ruler from ancient times. Read on for more descriptions of our Savior. Continue to underline as before.

> *He will stand and shepherd his flock in the strength of the LORD, in the majesty of the name of the LORD his God. And they will live securely, for then his greatness will reach to the ends of the earth. And he will be their peace. (Micah 5:4–5)*

_____

_____

4. The following two prophecies speak of the light for all. As you read and underline these passages, think back to how Jesus healed and liberated those held captive by sickness, demons, or sin.

> *I, the LORD, have called you in righteousness; I will take hold of your hand. I will keep you and will make you to be a covenant for the people and a light for the Gentiles, to open eyes that are blind, to free captives from prison and to release from the dungeon those who sit in darkness. (Isaiah 42:6–7)*
>
> *Nevertheless, there will be no more gloom for those who were in distress. In the past he humbled the land of Zebulun and the land of Naphtali, but in the future he will honor Galilee of the Gentiles, by the way of the sea, along the Jordan—The people walking in darkness have seen a great light; on those living in the land of the shadow of death a light has dawned. (Isaiah 9:1–2)*

Note your favorite phrase: _____

5. Continue underlining words of hope about the Savior.

> *In my vision at night I looked, and there before me was one like a son of man, coming with the clouds of heaven. He approached the Ancient of Days and was led into his presence. He was given authority, glory and sovereign power; all peoples, nations and men of every language worshiped him. His dominion is an everlasting*

dominion that will not pass away, and his kingdom is one that will never be destroyed. (Daniel 7:13–14)

The Old Testament points to our need for a Savior. God's chosen people longed for peace, safety, freedom, and justice. They wanted a King who would save them from persecution. How could they fathom that it was Jesus' own blood that would bring salvation?

Jesus' Words in Action: Jesus *was* the Word, *knew* the Word, *is* the Word, and *lived* the Word. Do we know the Word well enough for it to be a lamp unto our feet and a light unto our path (Psalm 119:105)? Jesus called Himself the Son of Man eighty times.[19] The Son of Man *will* return—that too has been prophesied. Do you realize that you pray through the Son of Man who sits at the right hand of God? I wonder what that looks like? Can you imagine it?

Wednesday: Testing and Trickery
Q and A

Jesus spends part of Monday through Thursday teaching in the temple. But His teaching is not without questioning. Unfortunately, the questions involve constant testing and trickery. Sometimes Jesus answers with another question, and sometimes Jesus answers with a parable. The interrogators' questions are intended to trap Jesus. Let's look at the Q and A sessions as if they are legal sparring. As you study each questioning session, look at *who* asked the question, *why* the question was asked, and *how* Jesus responds. Place yourself in the crowd of men and women listening to Jesus.

Scripture:	Questioner:	The Question/Why:	Jesus' Response:
1. Matthew 21:23–27 (Mark 11:27–33) (Luke 20:1–8)			
2. Matthew 22:15–22 (Mark 12:13–17) (Luke 20:20–26)			
3. Matthew 22:23–33 (Luke 20:27–40)			
4. Matthew 22:34–40 (Mark 12:28–34)			

And finally, Jesus has had enough. He lets loose! I wonder what it would feel like to be a woman in the audience hearing one of the most stinging, finger-pointing, and accusatory passages in the Bible, filled with name-calling. (I count at least 14)! If you're having one of those days when you need to vent, read Matthew 23:1–36.

Jesus' Words in Action: As you stood watching the Q and A ping-pong match, were the questions answered? Do you think the questioners asked from a burning desire to know Jesus? Jesus was the only answer they needed. Is Jesus the answer you want and need?

Thursday: The Hastening of the Hour

If you knew you had a week to live, what messages would you want to impart? A friend of mine with terminal breast cancer planned to videotape messages to her children. If I had to

> "Beware of the teachers of the law. They like to walk around in flowing robes and love to be greeted in the marketplaces and have the most important seats in the synagogues and the places of honor at banquets. They devour widows' houses and for a show make lengthy prayers. Such men will be punished most severely." (Luke 20:46–47)

teach my children a few last lessons, I'd want to caution and encourage them about each stage of life. I wouldn't waste time on anything unimportant. I'd want to leave a legacy of inspiration and faith.

Jesus must have wanted His last words to stick. He wanted His disciples to be prepared to continue without His physical presence and His male and female followers to remember the last lessons He taught. What follows is a list of Jesus' final lessons up until the Last Supper, excluding His prophecy, and the questioning by religious leaders already studied.

Place bookmarks in Matthew 21, Mark 11, Luke 19, and John 12 to simplify your research. In last week's skim-reading of the Gospels, you listed unfamiliar passages.

1. Choose three unfamiliar or intriguing events from the list below and write a key quote or point for it.

Last Lessons

Scripture:	Title of Event	Quote/Point
Matthew 21:18–19 (Mark 11:12–14)	Fig tree cursed	
Mark 11:15–19 (Luke 19:45–48)	The tables are turned	
Mark 11:20–25 (Matthew 21:19–22)	Witness of fig tree	
Matthew 21:28–32	Parable of the two sons	
Mark 12:1–12 (Matthew 21:33–45) (Luke 20:9–19)	Parable of the tenants	
Matthew 22:1–14	Parable of the wedding banquet	
Mark 12:28–34 (Matthew 22:34–40)	The greatest commandment	

Scripture:	Title of Event	Quote/Point
Matthew 23:37–39	Lament over Jerusalem	
Mark 12:41–44 (Luke 21:1–4)	The widow's gift	
Luke 21:5–36 (Mark 13:1–37) (Matthew 24:1–51)	Watch out!	
Matthew 25:1–12 Matthew 25:14–30 Matthew 25:31–46	Parable of the 10 virgins Parable of the talents Separating sheep and goats	
John 12:20–50	Prophecy fulfilled	
Matthew 26:1–5 (Mark 14:1–2) (Luke 22:1–2)	Crucifixion Prophecy	
John 12:1–8 (Matthew 26:6–13) (Mark 14:3–9)	Jesus is anointed (Saturday or Tuesday)	

Judas' Role

In John's account of Jesus' anointing by Mary of Bethany, Judas is indignant. Matthew and Mark both connect the anointing with Judas' betrayal. "Then Judas Iscariot, one of the Twelve, went to the chief priests to betray Jesus to them" (Mark 14:10; Matthew 26:14–15).

Why do you think Judas betrayed Jesus? Did he grasp who Jesus was? Was he annoyed with the extravagant anointing or was he frustrated with Jesus' battle plan? Was it for the money? Or was He pushing Jesus to claim His Kingship?

For whatever reason, Judas meets with the chief priests to betray Jesus (Matthew 26:14–16; Mark 14:10–11; Luke 22:3–6) and sets in motion the rest of our week. Though Judas may not seem to fit in with the story or with the other disciples, he does fit in with prophecy.

Even the thirty coins were prophesied in Exodus 21:32 as the slave price, and Old Testament Zechariah 11:12–13 states,

> I told them, "If you think it best, give me my pay; but if not, keep it." So they paid me thirty pieces of silver. And the LORD said to me, "Throw it to the potter"—the handsome price at which they priced me! So I took the thirty pieces of silver and threw them into the house of the Lord to the potter.

After the chief priests pay Judas thirty pieces, Judas attempts to return the money, knowing he has betrayed an innocent man. The blood money is rejected but instead used to purchase the *potter's field* as a burial place for foreigners. Judas then hangs himself.

In Acts, Peter gives us the final outcome of Judas, and ironically, where he died. When Judas hanged himself, he "fell headlong, his body burst open and all his intestines spilled out." The field is called Akeldama or Field of Blood. (Acts 1:16–20)

> "Then what was spoken by Jeremiah the prophet was fulfilled: 'They took the thirty silver coins, the price set on him by the people of Israel, and they used them to buy the potter's field, as the Lord commanded me.'" (Matthew 27:9–10)

Judas also fits right in with the figs and the temple. It is no accident that the fig tree episode is so closely aligned with the overturning of the tables in the temple. Both stories reveal little fruit on the vine. They promise something they don't deliver. What doesn't produce from the heart should be cut off. The temple's appearance also promises something it can't deliver. Similarly, the religious leaders *act* the part but have no heart in their actions. Judas has few fruits to demonstrate his faith. He is completely open for Satan to enter, tempt, and tear apart.[20]

The Cleansing of the Temple

To fully understand Jesus' wrath in the temple, we need to understand the temple system.

First, Roman coins with Caesar's image cannot be donated for temple tax; they have to be exchanged for Jewish coins. This allows for graft as moneychangers charged exorbitant rates to exchange coins.

Second, the unblemished animal brought for the sacrifice might not pass inspection. To be safe, Jews purchase a marked up lamb that has a greater chance of being declared fit for the sacrifice. These pre-certified sacrifices are high priced. Annas and Caiaphas are the beneficiaries in this moneymaking scheme and they do not want Jesus to ruin their business as usual. [21]

Third, the area filled with pens for sheep, cattle, goats, dove area, pots for sale, oil, salt, and wine booths, and booths for the money exchangers, may also be the Gentile area of worship. How could His Father's house be a house of prayer and worship for *all* people? Jesus doesn't like what He sees. [22]

Jesus' Words in Action: Which of these lessons pertains to you right now? Each day in the Word is new manna from heaven. Don't miss your food. Whenever you read Scripture, ask Jesus to reveal what you need to know. Stay tuned to His Word and keep your dial set to prayer.

> "For my house will be called a house of prayer for all nations." (Isaiah 56:7b)
>
> "Has this house, which bears my Name, become a den of robbers to you?" (Jeremiah 7:11a)
>
>

Friday: What Do the Disciples Know?

As we study the final week of Jesus' earthly life, let's consider what Jesus' listeners know. We know from our study of Mary Magdalene that she belongs to an inner circle of followers who hear prophecy and prayer. Do they understand how dangerously close they are to separation from their beloved teacher and friend?

Let's look at a few prophetic passages as well as *three* separate warnings Jesus gives to His disciples. You be the investigating lawyer. Just what do your clients know about the events leading up to the murder of Jesus Christ?

First, let's consider a parable. In Thursday's lesson about the hastening of the hour, we read a parable from Mark's Gospel about the owner of a vineyard who sends out servants at harvest time. They are all killed. At last he sends out his only son; He, too, is also murdered. This parable foreshadows Jesus' death as well as the Old Testament passage, which Jesus quotes.

Similarly, in a speech most likely delivered after Jesus cleansed the temple on Monday of Passion Week, Jesus prophesies His death.

📖 Read John 12:23–36.

1. Who is the kernel of wheat, and how does it produce more seeds (verse 24)?

_____

_____

> "The stone the builders rejected has become the capstone; the LORD has done this, and it is marvelous in our eyes." (Psalm 118:22–23)

Jesus then delivers what seems to be a paradox: Those who *love life will end up losing it.* Those who *hate life will inherit eternal life.* He also explains that serving means following (verse 26).

Jesus is not disturbed that the hour has come. Rather, he knows His purpose and that He must fulfill it.

2. What does Jesus say this is the time for (verses 31–32)?

_____

3. Who is the *prince of the world* and what will happen to him (verse 31)?

_____

_____

4. Jesus says in John 12:32, "When I am lifted up from the earth, [I] will draw all men to myself." What does he mean by being *lifted up*?

Besides this parable and teaching, Jesus prophesies at least three separate times about His death and resurrection. The synoptic Gospels record these prophecies. As you read the passages listed below in bold type, note the facts Jesus gives about His arrest, crucifixion, and resurrection.

> "The man who loves his life will lose it, while the man who hates his life in this world will keep it for eternal life." (John 12:25)
>

First Prediction: Read Mark 8:30—9:1 (Matthew 16:20–28; Luke 9:21–27).

5. What do the disciples learn about His death from His *first* prophecy?

_____

_____

Second Prediction: Read Matthew 17:22–23 (Mark 9:30–32; Luke 9:43–45).

6. What do the disciples learn about His death from His *second* prophecy?

_____

Luke adds a few interesting emotional elements to the story.

> *And they were all amazed at the greatness of God. While everyone was marveling at all that Jesus did, he said to his disciples, "Listen carefully to what I am about to tell you: The Son of Man is going to be betrayed into the hands of men." But they did not understand what this meant. It was hidden from them, so that they did not grasp it, and they were afraid to ask him about it. (Luke 9:43–45)*

7. How do the emotions change from the beginning to the end of Luke's passage?

_____

<u>Third Prediction</u>: Read Luke 18:31–34 (Matthew 20:17–19; Mark 10:32–34).

8. What new information does Luke give us about this third prediction?

_____

> They were on their way up to Jerusalem, with Jesus leading the way, and the disciples were *astonished*, while those who followed were *afraid*. Again he took the Twelve aside and told them what was going to happen to him. (Mark 10:32) ✤✝✤

9. Using all the accounts, put a check by the facts the disciples have been told.

- ❏ The Son of Man will be betrayed.
- ❏ Jesus will be rejected and suffer many things at the hands of religious leaders.
- ❏ The Son of Man will be handed over to the Gentiles.
- ❏ The Gentiles will mock, insult, spit, and flog him.
- ❏ The Son of Man will be condemned to death.
- ❏ The Son of Man will be lifted up from the earth.
- ❏ Jesus must be killed.
- ❏ Jesus will be raised to life on the third day.
- ❏ The Son of Man will come in His Father's glory and reward each man's work.

The answer is: all of the above. Does it make you want to ask the listeners how they could have failed to hear and understand? Jesus is so specific in these passages. And the fulfillment of the persecution passages is so deadly accurate. Why don't they believe He will rise again? Bible commentator Matthew Henry writes,

The disciples' prejudices were so strong, that they would not understand these things literally. They were so intent upon the prophecies which spake of Christ's glory, that they overlooked those which spake of his sufferings. People run into mistakes, because they read their Bibles by halves, and are only for the smooth things. We are as backward to learn the proper lessons from the sufferings, crucifixion, and resurrection of Christ, as the disciples were to what he told them as to those events; and for the same reason; self-love, and a desire of worldly objects, close our understandings.[23]

If the disciples are in denial about Jesus' death, they most likely close their eyes to their *own* rough roads ahead. Read on for what Jesus warns the disciples about their *own* futures. Underline what could have prompted questions or fears.

> *You must be on your guard. You will be handed over to the local councils and flogged in the synagogues. On account of me you will stand before governors and kings as witnesses to them. And the gospel must first be preached to all nations. Whenever you are arrested and brought to trial, do not worry beforehand about what to say. Just say whatever is given you at the time, for it is not you speaking, but the Holy Spirit. (Mark 13:9–11; see also Matthew 24:9–14; Luke 21:12–19)*

Other passages reveal Jesus' warnings to the disciples accompanied by the assurances not to worry because the Holy Spirit will teach them what to say when needed (Matthew 10:17–25; Luke 12:11–12). We will see this prophecy fulfilled in Week Eight's study of Pentecost.

Jesus' Words in Action: Jim Elliot, missionary to the Auca Indians in Ecuador, wrote in his journal, "He is no fool who gives what he cannot keep to gain what he cannot lose."

Jim Elliot couldn't have known then that in six years he would be murdered by the very people he was trying to save. After his death, his wife and others continued ministering to his murder-

> "If anyone would come after me, he must deny himself and take up his cross and follow me." (Matthew 16:24)

ers, and many came to salvation in Christ. Elliot's life is now the subject of the movie *The End of the Spear* and books *Through Gates of Splendor* and *Shadow of the Almighty*.

Though you may not lose your life for Christ, you are still a disciple who will be persecuted in His name and suffer on His account. But you will also share in His glory.

> *I tell you the truth, unless a kernel of wheat falls to the ground and dies, it remains only a single seed. But if it dies, it produces many seeds. The man who loves his life will lose it, while the man who hates his life in this world will keep it for eternal life. (John 12:24–25)*

Saturday: "There Is a Fountain Filled with Blood"

Scripture: "On that day a fountain will be opened to the house of David and the inhabitants of Jerusalem, to cleanse them from sin and impurity." (Zechariah 13:1)

"There Is a Fountain" rates as one of my favorite Lenten hymns with its simple melody and heartfelt words. Its repetition reinforces the most powerful phrases.

However, its lyricist did not lead a simple life. William Cowper was an English poet who struggled with depression and even attempted suicide. He was institutionalized in an insane asylum for eighteen months, where he read the Bible and became a Christian at the age of 33 (1764). "There is a Fountain" was just one of many poems he wrote.

Though he was not freed from his emotional torment, he wrote sixty-seven hymns for *Olyney Hymns*. Today, speak these words aloud or sing these verses unto the Lord. God has brought you close to Him through the blood of His Son.

"There Is a Fountain"

There is a fountain filled with blood drawn from Emmanuel's veins;
And sinners plunged beneath that flood lose all their guilty stains.
Lose all their guilty stains, lose all their guilty stains;
And sinners plunged beneath that flood lose all their guilty stains.

The dying thief rejoiced to see that fountain in his day;
And there have I, though vile as he, washed all my sins away.

Washed all my sins away, washed all my sins away;
And there have I, though vile as he, washed all my sins away.

Dear dying Lamb, thy precious blood shall never lose its power
Till all the ransomed church of God be saved, to sin no more.
Be saved, to sin no more, be saved, to sin no more;
Till all the ransomed church of God be saved, to sin no more.

Response: *Dear Jesus, I am a sinner but you have made me lose all my guilty stains. You have washed all my sins away. Your precious blood will never lose its power. For all who believe are saved forevermore. Thank you for your fountain. Thank you for Your blood which cleanses me.*

> Dear dying Lamb, thy precious blood shall never lose its power.
>
> "There is a Fountain" William Cowper

Sunday: "Nothing but the Blood"

Scripture: " 'Come now, let us reason together,' says the LORD. 'Though your sins are like scarlet, they shall be as white as snow; though they are red as crimson, they shall be like wool.'" (Isaiah 1:18)

"Nothing but the Blood" was one of the praise songs I led in Vacation Bible School one summer. Group Publishing took the simple gospel tune built on the first five notes of a scale and made it into a jammin' rap song. The kids especially loved it. Day Four of VBS focused on Jesus' death and resurrection, and on that day I learned it was more than rap that the kids loved.

The instructions said to begin without the CD, and to sing a cappella, "What can wash away my sins?" I began the solo and waited for the children to respond. It is a beautiful thing to hear one hundred children's voices sing out the answer, "Nothing but the Blood of Jesus."

There is only one answer to that question. Baptist pastor Robert Lowry wrote this song in the late 1800s, but it remains timeless because the answer will never change.

What can wash away my sin?	*Nothing but the blood of Jesus*
What can make me whole again?	*Nothing but the blood of Jesus*
For my pardon this I see	*Nothing but the blood of Jesus;*
For my cleansing, this my plea	*Nothing but the blood of Jesus*
Nothing can for sin atone	*Nothing but the blood of Jesus;*
Naught of good that I have done	*Nothing but the blood of Jesus*
This is all my hope and peace	*Nothing but the blood of Jesus*
This is all my righteousness	*Nothing but the blood of Jesus*

Chorus:
Oh! Precious is the flow that makes me white as snow
No other fount I know, nothing but the blood of Jesus

Response: *Lord, it is only by your blood that I am made white as snow. Wash me in the fount of your blood. Forgive my sins. May you be my hope, my peace and my righteousness. And may I never take for granted that my salvation is through nothing but the blood of Jesus.*

Works Cited

1. Maier, Paul L., *In the Fullness of Time: A Historian Looks at Christmas, Easter, and the Early Church* (Grand Rapids, MI: Kregel, 1991), 108.

2. *The MacArthur Study Bible* (Nashville, TN: Thomas Nelson, Word Publishing, 1997), 1554.

3. Ray Vander Laan and Focus on the Family Video (That the World May Know Series), *The True Easter Story and Lamb of God* (Grand Rapids, MI: Zondervan, 2000); Maier, 108.

4. Vander Laan and Focus on the Family Video, *The True Easter Story and Lamb of God*. "Messiah in Passover," http://biblicalholidays.com

5. Vander Laan and Focus on the Family Video, *The True Easter Story and Lamb of God*.

6. Deffinbaugh, Bob, "The Untriumphal Entry (Luke 19:28–44)," http://www.bible.org.

7. *The MacArthur Study Bible*, 1484.

8. Deffinbaugh, "The Triumphal Tragedy," http://www.bible.org.

9. *Harper's Bible Commentary*, in Accordance Bible software. CD-ROM, version 5.7. Oak Tree Software, Inc.

Easton's Bible Dictionary, in Accordance Bible software. CD-ROM, version 5.7. Oak Tree Software, Inc.

10. Vander Laan and Focus on the Family Video, *The True Easter Story and Lamb of God*.

Deffinbaugh, "The Untriumphal Entry (Luke 19:28–44), http://www.bible.org.

11. Vander Laan and Focus on the Family Video, *The True Easter Story and Lamb of God*.

12. Ibid.

13. Ibid.

14. *The MacArthur Study Bible*, 1438, 1554–1555.

15. *Matthew Henry Commentary*, in Accordance Bible software. CD-ROM, version 5.7. Oak Tree Software, Inc.

16. Lucado, Max, *The Final Week of Jesus* (Multnomah, OR: Multnomah Books, 1994), 21.

17. Ibid.

18. Bishop, Jim, *The Day Christ Died: The Inspiring Classic on the Last 24 Hours of Jesus' Life* (San Francisco: Harper, 1957), 55.

19. Lucado, 21.

20. Aycock, Don M., *Eight Days That Changed the World: A Devotional Study from Palm Sunday to Easter* (Grand Rapids, MI: Kregel, 1990), 30.

21. MacArthur, John, *The Murder of Jesus: A Study of How Jesus Died* (Nashville, TN: Thomas Nelson, 2000), 106–107.

22. Vander Laan and Focus on the Family Video (That the World May Know Series), *Faith Lessons on the Death and Resurrection of the Messiah: City of a Great King (1)* (Grand Rapids, MI: Zondervan, 1997, 1998), Volume 4, Video 1.

Deffinbaugh, "The Tempest in the Temple: The Abuses of Authority" (Luke 20:1–18), http://www.bible.org.

———, "The Triumphal Tragedy" (Mark 11:1–25), http://www.bible.org.

23. *Matthew Henry Commentary*, , in Accordance Bible software. CD-ROM, version 5.7. Oak Tree Software, Inc.

The Last Days

> "We all, like sheep, have gone astray, each of us has turned to his own way; and the LORD has laid on him the iniquity of us all." (Isaiah 53:6)

Last week we learned that Jesus entered Jerusalem *with* the Passover lambs *as* the Passover Lamb. Today we continue to see His significance as the *Lamb of God* as we study the background of two of the three major Jewish Spring Festivals: Passover and the Feast of the Unleavened Bread.

Monday: The Significance of the Lamb
Old Testament Traditions

The Lord promised the Hebrews freedom from their Egyptian bondage (Exodus 6:6–8).

Moses pleaded with Pharaoh to "Let my people go," but Pharaoh refused. After nine plagues that afflicted the Egyptians with bloody waters, frogs, lice, flies, disease, boils, hailstorm, locusts, and darkness, God chose to kill all the first-born sons in Egypt while *passing over* the Israelites.

Read Exodus 12:1–34 to discover the origin of Passover and the Feast of the Unleavened Bread.

1. Using the outline below, fill in the verse references for each topic.

Outline—Exodus 12:1–34

I. Preparations for *first Passover* given by God to Moses (verses_____)

II. Prophecy for Passover night (verses_____)

III. Preparations for *first Feast of Unleavened Bread* (verses_____)

IV. Preparations relayed by Moses to the people (verses_____)

V. Prophecy for Passover night fulfilled (verses_____)

2. Did God really need a marking on a door to let Him know where the Israelites lived? Of course He doesn't. So why do you think God required this sign?

_____

_____

3. What specifications were necessary for the sacrificial lamb or kid (Exodus 12:5)?

_____

_____

On our sheep farm we have witnessed birth and death. One year my sensitive first grader grieved the death of a struggling lamb. With tears in her eyes, Julia begged me for an answer. "Why did it have to die? It didn't do *anything* wrong!" I agreed with her. It seemed very unfair; the lamb had done nothing wrong. Neither had Jesus. He was the perfect, spotless, sinless lamb—who did absolutely nothing wrong. It took a perfect lamb to take away the sins of the world.

4. How long was the sacrificial lamb to live with the family (Exodus 12:3, 6)? Why were these days required?

_____

_____

The Passover lamb was chosen on the tenth day of the Hebrew month, *Nisan,* and it was slain on the fourteenth day. Between those days, the Passover lamb was kept and cared for in the house. Perhaps this made the sacrifice all the more difficult for the family. My experience has formed my opinion that few baby animals are as sweet as young lambs.

Old Testament Prophecy Fulfilled

"The next day John saw Jesus coming toward him and said, 'Look, the Lamb of God, who takes away the sin of the world!' " (John 1:29)

Each spring my heart delights in the first lamb. After the mother ewe has cleaned it, it stands on knobby knees and attempts to nurse. However, sometimes a lamb is weak or cold, or the mother cannot care for it. On these occasions, we warm the lamb in a lukewarm bath, blow-dry it, wrap it in a towel, and keep it in a warm place until we can return it to its mother. If the mother has died or rejects the lamb, the lamb becomes a bottle feeder. My daughters have taken bottle-feeders to school for show-and-tell. They become like cherished pets. My husband discourages us from naming the sheep because every named animal becomes special and painful to send to market. We usually try to give away our bottle feeders to friends who want a pet lamb. This avoids grief on market day when my daughters would have to say goodbye to a lamb we've bottle-fed four to six times a day for six weeks. How difficult it must have been to sacrifice that chosen lamb at Passover. It had a name—the name of the family for whom it was sacrificed.

5. What time of day was the animal to be slaughtered (12:6)?

_____

6. What else was to be included in the dinner (Exodus 12:8)?

_____

God explains that in seeing the blood, "I will pass over you," and concluded with the instruction that this day of commemoration and remembrance shall continue (verses 13–14).

When Moses forwarded the instructions to the people, He told them to take hyssop and dip it in blood, then when the Lord went through the land He would pass over that doorway, and would not permit the destroyer to enter their houses and strike them down (see Exodus 12:22–23). Wouldn't that sound reassuring? We have that same assurance with the blood of Jesus Christ. Instead of one lamb for each family of ten or so, we have the *One* Lamb for all who will believe!

When my youngest daughter Julia was a toddler, she pointed to one lambie and said, "Mommy, that one doesn't have its price tag!" I laughed, because none of them had a "price tag"! They had *ear tags*. But it made me think. Jesus the Lamb of God had a huge price tag on Him. No one could ever determine the infinite value of saving all the believers for eternity. The price was His life, a huge cost. How much would you pay for eternity? Infinite value, and yet it's free for the asking.

Over a thousand years later, the celebration of Passover continued. Let's see what it looked like in Jesus' time.

Passover began with a prayer of sanctification

> For you know that it was not with perishable things such as silver or gold that you were redeemed from the empty way of life handed down to you from your forefathers, but with the precious blood of Christ, a lamb without blemish or defect (1 Peter 1:18–19).

(*qiddus*), the first cup, and the serving of the first course of bitter and green herbs. After the second cup was poured, the head of the household explained the parts of the meal, which was followed by the liturgy, "And when your children ask you, 'What does this ceremony mean to you?'" (Exodus 12:26), they had a time of remembrance. The story or *haggadah* was told, and then participants sang Psalm 113 and drank the second cup.

The main meal followed, with a benediction for the unleavened bread, lamb (sacrifice for sins), and bitter herbs (bitterness of captivity). Some ceremonies now add a hard-boiled egg and charoseth, a fruit and nut chutney symbolizing the mortar Hebrews used to make bricks during their captivity.

> "...for all have sinned and fall short of the glory of God, and are justified freely by his grace through the redemption that came by Christ Jesus. God presented him as a sacrifice of atonement, through faith in his blood." (Romans 3:23–25a)

They drank cup number three, the cup of blessing, and then the Passover meal ended with singing Psalms 115—118 and a benediction for the fourth (Hallel) cup.[1]

Christ's sacrifice on the cross as the *Lamb of God* has made the *Passover* Lamb forever unnecessary. Bible Commentator Matthew Henry encourages us to spend all of our days remembering God's work through the ages and finds the *last* Passover a more important night than the *first*. "Then a yoke, heavier than that of Egypt, was broken from off our necks, and a land, better than that of Canaan, set before us. It was a redemption to be celebrated in heaven, for ever and ever."[2]

Christ's final passover introduces the first Lord's Supper

Jesus' Words in Action: God put a priority on remembering and celebrating freedom. Do you celebrate what God has done in your life? Do you remind others of God's goodness and grace throughout the years? Do you retell and *pass on* the Bible stories that reveal God's faithfulness?[3] You now have a freedom much greater than the freedom from bondage celebrated by the Hebrew people.

And when you celebrate communion, can you grasp its significance? When your children ask, "What does this ceremony mean?" can you answer? Do you understand you are sharing the blessing of Christ's blood and the benefits of His body (see 1 Corinthians 10:16)? You have so much to celebrate!

Tuesday: The Last Passover

How many times have we experienced the Lord's Supper and heard the familiar words, "This is my blood of the covenant, which is poured out for many" (Mark 14:24). But what if it were the very *first* time you heard those words? What if during a familiar ceremony, *unfamiliar* phrases flowed? Today try to witness this *Last Passover* for the *first* time.

> "As you know, the Passover is two days away—and the Son of Man will be handed over to be crucified." (Matthew 26:2)
>
>

On Tuesday of Passover Week, Jesus tells the disciples the clock is ticking down. If they listen attentively, the timeline should be clear.

On Thursday, Jesus asks His disciples to prepare for Passover. This will be a Passover like no other, a Passover to end all Passovers—literally. For Christians, Passover becomes the *Last* Supper to be replaced by the *Lord's* Supper.

📖 Read Luke 22:7–13 (compare to Matthew 26:17–19; Mark 14:12–16). Place bookmarks at Luke 22, John 13, and Mark 14.

1. Who are the only individuals "in the know"? Why do you think some of the other disciples are not given these directions?

_____

The details are left to Jesus' closest disciples. Judas is not informed of the destination for Passover, perhaps to prevent an early betrayal. Jesus needs quality time with His disciples.[4] Finding the location is simplified because women usually carry the water. So a man carrying it would be an obvious sign. Peter and John's responsibilities include securing a lamb between the ages of eight days and one year, purchasing herbs, spices, and bread, cleansing the home of leaven, cooking unleavened bread, and sacrificing the lamb like every Jewish male does in a fifteen-mile radius around Jerusalem.[5]

For the Passover celebration, circa AD 30, the *shofar* is blown at 3:00 p.m., when lambs are sacrificed. The sacrifices continue until 5:00 p.m. (twilight). If everyone in these regions observed Passover the same way, than nearly a quarter of a million lambs would have to be slain in a two-hour window of time. That would necessitate six hundred priests killing four lambs per minute. However, because the Pharisees, Galilean Jews, and Northern residents celebrate Passover from sunrise to sunrise, they sacrifice on Thursday. Sadducees, residents of Jerusalem, and other districts around Jerusalem celebrate from sundown to sundown and thus sacrifice on Friday. This spreads out the sacrificing to two days[6] and allows Jesus to both *celebrate* Passover as well as *to offer Himself as* the Passover Lamb.[7]

📖 Read John 13:1–11—The Washing of the Disciples' Feet.

2. John 13:3 states: "Jesus knew that the Father had put _____ _____ under _____ _____, and that he had come from _____ and was returning to _____;"

3. Then verse 4 continues with *"SO he got up from the meal...."* Why the connection?

_____

_____

Washing feet was customary; the lowest slaves were asked (though they could not be commanded) to do this job.[8] Jesus has one more night to show this group of men, who fight to be greatest, what it means to serve. He begins to show them the "full extent of his love" (verses 1, 4, 5) by washing their feet.

> "For even the Son of Man did not come to be served, but to serve, and to give his life as a ransom for many." (Mark 10:45)

4. What happens if Peter is not washed (verse 8)?

_____

After Jesus explains the absolute necessity of the cleansing, Peter exclaims that he doesn't just want his *feet* washed, but his *hands* and *head* as well (verse 9)! Remember this outcry, because Jesus is just about to warn Peter that he will deny Him.

Jesus tells them He has "eagerly desired to eat this Passover" with His disciples before He suffers (Luke 22:15). During the meal, Judas' betrayal is also prophesied.

📖 Read Mark 14:18–21 (also Matthew 26:21–25; Luke 22:21–23).

5. Who asks if they might be the betrayer (Mark 14:19)?

Can you imagine how you might feel if your fingers were in the bowl at the moment Jesus said, "one who dips bread into the bowl with me?" (Mark 14:21)

There is no question that Jesus is in control of the evening's events and nothing—not even the betrayal—is a surprise to Him. After the third cup, the cup of redemption, Jesus inserts something new into the familiar Passover ceremony and this is a surprise to the disciples.

Read Luke 22:17–20—The Lord's Supper (Matthew 26:26–29, Mark 14:22–25).

In the middle of this Passover Feast known as the Last Supper, after taking a cup and giving thanks, Jesus introduces a "new covenant." In one of the episodes of Ray Vander Laan's *That the World May Know* video series, he states that engagement and marriage feasts during Christ's time contained references to a "new covenant." In engagement ceremonies of this time, after the bride price has been negotiated by both sets of parents, a cup of wine is poured for the son. The son then offers the cup to his bride-to-be and asks her to accept his "new covenant" represented in the marriage agreement terms. Drinking from the cup symbolized the bride's formal acceptance of the marriage proposal and all the good and bad circumstances that come with marriage. According to Vander Laan, when Christ mentions "a new covenant" during this Passover occasion, the disciples most likely associated these three words with the wedding customs of the times. Through the illustration of a man's love and devotion for his bride, they gained at least a nebulous comprehension of Christ's unswerving love and devotion for them and for all who follow Him.[9]

"This is my blood of the covenant, which is poured out for many." (Mark 14:24)

Read Luke 22:24–38.

6. What topic do the disciples bicker about (Luke 22:24)?

7. Jesus' words mirror His actions, "The _____ among you

should be like the _____, and the one who _____ like the one who
_____. For who is _____, the one who is at the _____ or
the one who _____? Is it not the one who is at the table? But I am
among you as the one who _____" (Luke 22:26–27).

Jesus' Words in Action: The next time you read
1 Corinthians 11:23–29 or experience communion, consider
Jesus' invitation to accept the cup of His new covenant. Each
time you celebrate the Lord's Supper, consider His beautiful
invitation. Are you part of His bride? Are you longing for your
groom's return? How can we demonstrate our longing in practical ways of living?

Wednesday: The Calm Before the Storm
　　　　　　Last Words at the Last Supper

It is nearly time for Jesus to say goodbye to his disciples.
Listen for His love and fatherly caring. He will call them *my
children* and assure them that He will not leave them as
orphans. Oh, how great is His love and how He longs for them
to be unified in love.

📖 Read John 13:30–38; 14:1–27.

1. Fill in the words from the new commandment. "A new
command I give to you: _____ one another. As I have
_____ you, so you must _____ _____ _____. By this ___
____ will know that you are my _____, if you ____ one
another" (John 13:34–35).

2. In these final moments, the disciples have some individual questions. In your own words, write each man's questions, and then add your own question. What might *you* have
asked? Has Jesus answered your question?

Name:	Question/Comment:	Answers:
Peter (13:36–37)		
Thomas (14:5)		
Philip (14:8)		
Judas (Not Iscariot) (14:22)		

_____
(your name)

Jesus' responses are powerful. One way He comforts follows His prophecy of Peter's denial. He says to the disciples, "And if I go and prepare a place for you, I will come back and take you to be with me that you also may be where I am" (John 14:3).

As He did during the Passover meal, Jesus uses verbiage from the betrothal ceremony. After the groom offers the cup to the bride and she accepts the cup, he says he will go and prepare a place for her; the groom uses the words Jesus said to the disciples in the garden of Gethsemane (John 14:3).

The groom prepares a place for his bride by adding rooms onto his father's home. This betrothal time could last up to twelve months. When the *father* feels the home is ready, he alerts the son to go to his bride. The wedding party, including the bridesmaids with their lamps full of oil, proceeds to the home of the bride. When the "best man" announces their arrival with the blowing of the shofar, the bride dresses for the occasion and runs to greet her groom.[10]

Jesus uses the marriage picture to depict what is happening at His departure. He's readying heaven for believers on earth. He leaves to prepare a place for us where we will live in community, but He will return. Will our lamps be burning? Will we run to greet our bridegroom?

> "In my Father's house are many rooms; if it were not so, I would have told you. I am going there to prepare a place for you. And if I go and prepare a place for you, I will come back and take you to be with me that you also may be where I am." (John 14:2–3)

3. Read John 14:1–4 and list the points He makes to comfort them.

Don't be troubled; trust God.

4. Read John 14:16–21 and add to the points He makes to comfort them.

Between these words of comfort, Jesus delivers one of His "I AM" statements.

Fill in the blanks below:

"I am the _____ and the _____ and the _____. ___ _____ comes to the _____ except through _____. If you really _____ me, you would _____ my _____ as well. From now on, you do _____ him and have _____ him." (John 14:5–7)

Many people want to believe that all religions lead to God. But Jesus claims there is NO way to the Father except *through* Him. If we believe in Jesus and His words, we cannot be vague about the one way to salvation. He wouldn't have needed to die on the cross if there were many other ways.

6. According to John 14:15, 21, and 23, LOVE =
_____.

And finally, Jesus predicts His second coming. He promises the Holy Spirit, which is the Spirit of Truth and a counselor who will be with them forever.

7. In John 14:25–26 Jesus reveals what the Holy Spirit can do. List these points below.

_____

_____

8. Jesus continues to comfort as a father. Memorize this next verse and recall it the next time your heart is anxious.

" _____ I leave with you; my _____ I give you. I do not give to you as the world gives. Do not let your hearts be _____ and do not be _____." (John 14:27)

We'll conclude today's study with Jesus' words as they leave Passover for Gethsemane.

📖 Read John 14:28–31.

What should the disciples understand by these words? Put yourself in their sandals.

Because of His love for the Father and because of His love for each of these disciples and us, He will lay down His life. This is His choice. Oh, those heavy last five words: *"Come now; let us leave"* (verse 31). These words mean so much more to Jesus than to His followers. Jesus leaves the communion of friends to journey to where they will desert Him. This is the beginning of the end.

Jesus' Words in Action: Jesus' final messages are about peace ("Peace I leave with you") and love ("Love one another"). How do you follow that new commandment? Will others recognize by your love that you are a disciple? Jesus chose to love us even while we were sinners. How can you reach out with unconditional and sacrificial love so others will know you are a Christian?

The Drama of the Passion

Gethsemane to Golgotha in 13 Scenes

Scene One

Title: The sheep and the rooster
Reference: ***Matthew 26:30–35***
Location: *Walking to Mount of Olives*
Characters: *Jesus, disciples (not Judas)*

Scene Two

Title: Jesus' last words and prayers
References: ***John 15, 16, 17***
Scene: *Walking to Kidron Valley*
Characters: *Jesus, disciples, (not Judas)*

Scene Three

Title: Jesus prays/disciples sleep
Reference: ***Mark 14:32–42***
(Matthew 26:36–46; Luke 22:40–46)
Location: *Gethsemane: Olive grove*
Characters: *Jesus, Peter, James, John*

Scene Four

Title: Jesus is arrested
Reference: ***John 18:2–12***
(Matthew 26:47–56; Mark 14:43–49; Luke 22:47–54)
Location: *Gethsemane: Olive grove*
Characters: *Jesus, disciples, Roman soldiers, Jewish officials, Malchus, Judas*

Scene Five (Religious Trial #1)

Title: Jesus before Annas
Reference: ***John 18:12b–24***
Location: *Home of Annas/Courtyard*
Characters: *Jesus, Annas, members of Sanhedrin, John, Peter, servant girl*
*Meanwhile, Peter denies Jesus the first time

Scene Six (Religious Trial #2)

Title: "I AM" before Caiaphas
Reference: ***Mark 14:55–65***
(Matt 26:59–68; Luke 22:63–65)
Location: *Home of Caiaphas/ Courtyard*
Characters: *Jesus, chief priests, Sanhedrin, guards, Peter*
**Meanwhile Peter denies Jesus the second time (Matthew 26:69–72; Luke 22:55–58)
***Peter denies Jesus the 3rd time (Luke 22:59–62)
(Matthew 26:73–75; Mark 14:70b–72; John 18:26–27)

Scene Seven (Religious Trial #3)

Title: "I AM" before the council
Reference: ***Luke 22:66–71***
Location: *Perhaps high priests' home*
Characters: *Jesus, council of the elders, chief priests, teachers of the law*
**Judas remorsefully returns to chief priests (Matthew 27:3–10)

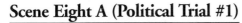

Scene Eight A (Political Trial #1)

Title: Jesus before Pilate
Reference: **John 18:28–32**
(Matthew 27:2; Luke 23:1–2)
Location: *Outside Praetorium*
Characters: *Pilate and the Jews*

Scene Eight B

Title: The King before Pilate
Reference: **John 18:33–38**
*(Matthew 27:11–14;
Mark 15:2–5; Luke
23:3,4)*
Location: *Inside/Outside Praetorium*
Characters: *Jesus, Pilate, Jews*

Scene Nine (Political Trial #2)

Title: Jesus before Herod
Reference: **Luke 23:5–12**
Location: *Herod's Palace*
Characters: *Jesus, Herod, chief priests,
teachers of the law, soldiers*

Scene Ten (Political Trial #3)

Title: Jesus or Barabbas?
References: **Luke 23:13–16, Mark
15:6–14**
*(Matthew 27:15–23; John
18:39–40)*
Location: *Praetorium*
Characters: *Jesus, Barabbas, Pilate,
chief priests, crowd*
**Pilate's wife sends Pilate a
concerned warning (Matthew 27:19)

Scene Eleven

Title: Jesus is persecuted.
Reference: **Matthew 27:27–30**
*(John 19:1–3; Mark
15:16–19)*
Location: *Praetorium*
Characters: *Jesus, Pilate, governor's sol-
diers*

Scene Twelve

Title: "Crucify! Crucify!
Reference: **John 19:4–17**
*(Matthew 27:24–26, 31;
Luke 23:24–25)*
Location: *Inside/Outside Praetorium*
Characters: *Jesus, crowd, Pilate, chief
priests, Barabas*

Scene Thirteen

Title: Journey to the Cross
Reference: **Luke 23:26–31; Mark
15:21–22**
Location: *Way of Sorrows*
Characters: *Jesus, women, crowd, sol-
diers, Simon of Cyrene*

Thursday: The Garden of Gethsemane

Max Lucado writes in *The Final Week of Jesus,* "The final battle was won in Gethsemane. . . . For it was in the garden that he made his decision. He would rather go to hell for you than go to heaven without you."[11]

The Last Supper is the beginning of the end. It provides Jesus with the "food" He needs to do the will of God and finish His work. Jesus knows it is time to do what He had been sent to do. I hope you're able to finish your work today, too! It's a long day of study, but it was a long night for Jesus.

Look at the chart on pages 126–127, where you will find the final thirteen scenes of Jesus' life depicted in **The Drama of the Passion: Gethsemane to Golgotha.** This is your road map complete with location, characters, and references. For the next few days you will refer to these pages and read the bold references to better understand the sequence of events.

Now let's walk from Jerusalem to the Mount of Olives. To get there, you will have to cross the Kidron Valley. The moon is full and illuminates the Kidron Brook, which is red with the sacrificial blood of at least a hundred thousand Passover Lambs flowing from the altar down a strait to the brook.[12] What is going through Jesus' mind with that visual reminder of sacrifice?

1. Now read Matthew 26:30–35, the reference for Scene 1 from the Drama of the Passion flow chart.

Jesus both warns and encourages Simon Peter, "Simon, Simon, Satan has asked to sift you as wheat. But I have prayed for you, Simon, that your faith may not fail. And when you have turned back, strengthen your brothers" (Luke 22:31–32).

Simon is shocked to think that he would ever deny Jesus. "Lord, I am ready to go with you to prison and to death" (Luke 22:33). "Even if all fall away, I will not" (Mark 14:29). But Jesus knows the future and gives Simon a preview. "Today— yes, tonight—before the rooster crows twice you yourself will disown me three times" (Mark 14:30).

Peter isn't through arguing, "Even if I have to die with you, I will never disown you" (Mark 14:31).

As the disciples travel to the Mount of Olives, they sing a hymn (see Mark 14:26). The chosen hymn might have been from Psalms 115—118 because of its connection with the Passover.

2. Read the verses from these psalms below and pretend you are the disciples. <u>Underline</u> portions that would be meaningful to Jesus and His disciples in their situation.

The LORD is my strength and my song; he has become my salvation.

Shouts of joy and victory resound in the tents of the righteous:

"The LORD's right hand has done mighty things!

The LORD's right hand is lifted high; the LORD's right hand has done mighty things!"

I will not die but live, and will proclaim what the LORD has done.

The LORD has chastened me severely, but he has not given me over to death (Psalm 118:14–18).

I will lift up the cup of salvation and call on the name of the LORD.

I will fulfill my vows to the LORD in the presence of all his people.

Precious in the sight of the LORD is the death of his saints.

O LORD, truly I am your servant; I am your servant, the son of your maidservant; you have freed me from my chains.

I will sacrifice a thank offering to you and call on the name of the LORD.

I will fulfill my vows to the LORD in the presence of all his people,

in the courts of the house of the LORD—in your midst, O Jerusalem. Praise the LORD (Psalm 116:13–19).

> "The stone the builders rejected has become the capstone; the LORD has done this, and it is marvelous in our eyes." (Psalm 118:22–23)

In this same scene, Jesus forewarns his disciples using Old Testament prophecy from Zechariah 13:7.

Now the action moves to Scene Two as Jesus and his disciples walk to the Kidron Valley. This is one of my favorite scenes in the Bible. These are Jesus' last words to His disciples before His arrest. These words were meant to last; they are full of metaphors and instruction. In this section, Jesus explains that He is the vine and we are the branches and teaches about love. Yesterday we talked of *love* and *peace*. Today we'll talk of *joy*.

Skim-Read John 15:1–16, and look for the answers to the following questions.

3. List benefits and negatives below.

Remaining In Jesus/Vine (verses 2,5,7,8)	Not remaining in Him (verses 2, 4, 5, 6)

4. Jesus obeyed His Father's commands and remained in His love (John 15:10).

We are to _____ Jesus' commands and to _____ in His love so that His _____ may be in us and our _____ will be _____ (John 15:10–11).

Then, as if the disciples might not have understood the foot washing, and as if they might not have heard His new command, Jesus repeats, "Love each other as I have loved you (John 15:12). Then He says again, "This is my command: Love each other" (John 15:17). But this is no *ordinary* love.

5. When Jesus speaks of love, His love is sacrificial. What do you think is going through the disciples' minds when they hear Jesus say "Greater love has no one than this, that he lay down his life for his friends" (John 15:13)?

_____

"Strike the shepherd, and the sheep will be scattered, and I will turn my hand against the little ones." (Zechariah 13:7)

Have you ever considered how unjoyful a situation is when we are outside of God's will and not obeying Him?

When you read through John in Week Four, you discovered many chapters devoted to Jesus' final dialogue with the disciples. Scene Two on the flow chart (Jesus' Last Words and Prayers) includes John 15:17–27 and John 16 dealing with persecution and the gift of the Holy Spirit.

In this passage, Jesus opens with "Love one another" but follows with a warning about the world's hate. I wonder if we need to understand love in the Christian community so we can stand strong in the world? Jesus warns that if the world hates us, remember it hated Him first.

_____

_____

6. Write John 15:18–19 in your own words so that you can apply it today.

_____

_____

7. According to John 15:26; 16:8–15, what else does the Holy Spirit do?

_____

_____

The disciples are clueless about Jesus' departure (John 16:16–18). He compares the separation and reunion to the pain of childbirth (John 16:19–24)! Though it's hard to imagine my husband understanding what it felt like to deliver our girls, when my daughter asks, "Did it hurt?" I can honestly say, "I'd do it tomorrow for another baby!" We rejoice in the new life we have in Christ as we do with a new life in our family.

If ever there were any doubt about where He came from and where He was going, Jesus makes it very clear in John 16:28. "I came from the Father and entered the world; now I am leaving the world and going back to the Father." And at hearing those words, the disciples understand! "This makes us believe that you came from God" (John 16:30).

"You believe at last!" (John 16:31) Jesus answers, but He goes on to forewarn them they will be scattered and all alone (verse 32). Why does He tell them these things? For the *same* reason He tells *us*.

How many times do *we* need to remember the end of the story? Take heart; *before* He was crucified, He knew He had overcome the world!

Now let's move on to the last chapter of this scene. Can you see that John has certainly recorded a great deal of additional information not mentioned in the other Gospels? What's the last thing the disciples see Jesus do before He is arrested? They see Him pray. This entire next chapter is a prayer. Note in John 17:5 where it says Jesus existed before the world began.

📖 Skim-read John 17 (conclusion of Scene 2) looking for the sections below.

> "I have told you these things, so that in me you may have peace. In this world you will have trouble. But take heart! I have overcome the world." (John 16:33)
>

I. Glorify Your Son (1–5)

II. I explained God to the disciples (6–10)

III. Protect the disciples, give them joy, sanctify them (11–19)

IV. I pray for unity for ALL believers (that includes all of us!) (20–26)[13]

📖 Read Mark 14:32–42 (Scene Three), your final reading for the day!

> "And now, Father, glorify me in your presence with the glory I had with you before the world began." (John 17:5)

Jesus prays in the Garden of Gethsemane, a garden of olive trees. The olive tree is the Messianic tree. Kings, priests, and prophets were anointed with olive oil. If an olive tree were cut down, out of the stump a new branch would grow. Similarly, Jesus of Nazareth (*netzer* = branch) is the new shoot bearing fruit and life.[14]

The word "Gethsemane" means "olive press." While in the garden, Jesus Himself is pressed so hard by anxiety and fear that His capillaries burst and he excretes blood in His sweat, a condition known as hematridosis. Isn't it interesting that it is Dr. Luke who mentions it in Luke 22:44?[15]

8. Who has Jesus specifically asked to be with Him as He prays (verse 33), and what reason does he give for prayer (Matthew 26:41)?

_____

_____

> "Watch and pray so that you will not fall into temptation. The spirit is willing, but the body is weak." (Matthew 26:41)

9. Jesus then pleads with the Father regarding the cup and His Father's will (Mark 14:36). What is the cup that Christ dreads?

_____

John MacArthur in *The Murder of Jesus* answers that question this way. "Clearly, what Christ dreaded most about the cross—the cup from which He asks to be delivered if possible—was the outpouring of divine wrath He would have to endure from His holy Father."[16] MacArthur further describes this scene as one of *sorrow, supplication and submission.*[17]

Jesus chose to drink of the cup. He prayed for *you* and drank the cup for *you* knowing everything you have done and will do in your life. What undying love He exhibits while under pressure in the Garden!

Jesus' Words in Action: The first verse in *"Go to Dark Gethsemane"* by James Montgomery is about the scene you've just studied.

Go to dark Gethsemane, ye that feel the tempter's power;
Your Redeemer's conflict see, watch with him one bitter hour;
Turn not from his griefs away, learn of Jesus Christ to pray.

> "The reason my Father loves me is that I lay down my life—only to take it up again.
>
> No one takes it from me, but I lay it down of my own accord." (John 10:17–18a)

The ending line of each verse lists something we should learn from Jesus: *"Learn of Jesus Christ to pray." "Learn of him to bear the cross,"* and *"Learn of Jesus Christ to die."* What do you learn from Jesus about the importance of prayer? Remember, He prayed for you in the garden (John 17:20–26).[18]

Friday: **When Jesus Looks at You**

The Arrest, Interrogation, Persecution (Part I)

I.N.R.I. Roman letters
Iesus Nazarenus Rex Iudaeorum
(Jesus of Nazareth, the King of the Jews)

Today we will read scenes four through seven and move from Jesus' arrest to His trials by the religious leaders. Every time Jesus enters a new scene, try to place yourself there with the characters. See Jesus in the scene.

Place bookmarks at John 18, Mark 14, Luke 22.

📖 Read John 18:2–12 (Scene Four).

1. Who shows up to arrest Jesus (verses 2–3)?

_____

2. What literally knocks the soldiers off their feet (John 18:6)? Why are those words powerful?

_____

In Matthew 26:53, Jesus explains He could have called on twelve legions of angels. Since a legion equals six thousand soldiers, this means seventy-two thousand angels![19] God's army is a lot bigger than any human army, but Jesus doesn't intend to do battle with clubs and swords. Jesus came in peace, as we will see with His healing in the Garden (Luke 22:51).

One year I witnessed the Garden of Gethsemane scene in our local Passion Play from a new and profound perspective. The play depicts Jesus praying, the soldiers and religious leaders arriving to arrest Jesus, and then Peter cutting off the slave Malchus' ear.

My seven-year-old nephew, Tim, came with us and ran from scene to scene, wriggling to the front to catch all the action. Now at the Garden, I could see Jesus and the servant, as well as my nephew wearing his ear-cap to protect his ear after his most recent surgery.

When Tim was born, I had watched the birth video and how the nurse gently explained to his adoring first-time parents that Tim's ear was deformed. Tim had a miniature, deformed ear with no hole. With medical advances in hearing repair, my brother and his wife opted for Tim to have multiple surgeries. Doctors created an ear from skin and cartilage from other areas on his body, and they would one day drill a hole in his skull.

Tim focused on the servant's bloodied ear and the gentle Jesus. I will never forget Tim's look of awe and surprised joy as He watched Jesus heal the servant, Jesus' last miracle before the miracle of the cross. With a slow realization, Tim connected with that wounded youth as well as the gentle and healing Jesus who came to bring peace, not the sword. Can you, too, connect with the Healer in the Garden?

By the end of the scene, Jesus is alone. This evening began with lessons of love and unselfish actions and now concludes with all the disciples fleeing and deserting Christ (see Matthew 26:56b). At some point Peter and another disciple (probably John) get up enough nerve to follow Jesus and his captors to find out what is happening to their Lord (John 18:15). This takes us to the beginning of His religious trials and scenes 5, 6, and 7.

Read John 18:12b–24 (Scene Five).

Caiaphas and Annas direct the religious trials. As in-laws and religious leaders, they probably live in the same large facility, their rooms separated by a courtyard.[20] They also share a problem: they want Jesus sentenced to death for blasphemy, but the Romans won't execute a person for those reasons alone. However, Romans *will* execute for sedition or insurrection.[21] Now the religious leaders need to make the *crime* fit the *punishment* of death.

Jesus will endure six trials, three by religious leaders and three by political leaders.[22] In these trials, almost all the rules will be broken. Truly, this *should* have been a mistrial except that nothing is a mistake with God.

Consider these rules as you watch Jesus undergo the trials:

- No night arrests or night trials
- Trials should recess until morning
- No trials on Feast Days or the Sabbath
- Trials should be held in Hall of Hewn Stone—Temple (not High Priests' residence)
- Trials must be public
- The accused should be considered innocent until proven guilty
- Must be indicted before arraigned (i.e., formally charged before being brought to court)
- Charges must be brought from *outside* the council
- The accused must have representation/defense, witnesses, and evidence
- The accused must not be hit or spat upon
- Witnesses must have precise testimony, dates, times, locations
- False witnesses could receive the death sentence
- Trial should last 2–3 days and include fasting
- If condemned, *must* be a *two-day* trial, and must have a revote[23]

> "Why do the nations conspire and the peoples plot in vain? The kings of the earth take their stand and the rulers gather together against the LORD and against his Anointed One." (Psalm 2:1–2)
>
>

As we look at Scenes 5, 6, and 7, let's also follow Peter and Judas. If I were directing a stage production of these events, I'd have the curtain closed and have Peter's first two denials occur in front of the curtain while the set changes to Caiaphas' room. Peter would be questioned and deny knowing the Messiah. At last, he would flee off stage and we'd open to the next scene with Caiaphas, Jesus, and the Sanhedrin, which is what we'll examine right now.

📖 Read Mark 14:55–65 (Scene Six—Religious Trial #2).

A few witnesses make false accusations regarding Jesus' statements about the temple (Mark 14:58). Just when *did* Jesus make the claim about tearing down the temple? Actually it was made way back in John 2:18–21 when Jesus spoke about destroying the temple of His *body*. "Destroy this temple, and I will raise it again in three days." But these false accusers claim His words were about the temple in Jerusalem, and still their testimonies do not agree.[24]

Then when Jesus is asked if He is the Christ, and the Son of the Blessed One, Jesus responds, "*I am.*" But He goes on to say they will see the Son of Man coming on the clouds of heaven (Mark 14:61–62). Jesus is quoting prophecy here and claims to be the One who was prophesied about in Daniel 7:13–14. Predictably, the high priest goes berserk over this. What about the high priest's meltdown and drama-king maneuver? According to Leviticus 21:10, he isn't supposed to do that.[25] But then again, *nobody* in this trial proceeding is doing anything the way it is supposed to be done.

📖 Read Luke 22:66–71 (Scene Seven).

When asked if He is the Son of God, Jesus answers, "You are right in saying I am" (Luke 22:70). Indeed! He is the Son of God, and He is the great I Am.

Perhaps one of the most horrendous scenes in the Bible is when a high priest's servant (a relative of the man Peter cut) recognizes Peter's involvement and accuses Peter. As a tortured Jesus is taken from one room to another, Peter denies Jesus in Jesus' presence.

Peter sees a beaten, interrogated man who loves Him more than anyone in the world. That man looks deep into his eyes and soul at the moment Peter denies Him.[26] What did those eyes look like? Will Peter ever forget them?

In various scenes, Luke is the writer who captures Peter's reactions. In Luke 22:54 we learn that when Jesus is arrested,

> "The high priest, the one among his brothers who has had the anointing oil poured on his head and who has been ordained to wear the priestly garments, must not let his hair become unkempt or tear his clothes." (Leviticus 21:10)

Peter follows at a distance, and after His denial with Jesus watching, Luke reveals that Peter "went outside and wept bitterly" (Luke 22:62).

For a minute, pretend that you're Peter. We've all denied the Lord, we've all sinned, and we've all chosen the sword instead of peace. What if every time we did something wrong we saw the disappointed face of Jesus? What if the Holy Spirit crowed a warning for us, and we allowed ourselves to hear it?

As we move closer to the cross, will you remember that Christ knew the cup He was accepting, and that He accepted this cup for you? He already knew everything you were going to do, and He still went to the cross.

> "The Lord turned and looked straight at Peter. Then Peter remembered the word the Lord had spoken to him: 'Before the rooster crows today, you will disown me three times.'" (Luke 22:61)

Jesus' Words in Action: At an Easter retreat, I asked each woman to draw a picture of herself at the cross or write words that could later become a poem or a song. One woman was gripped by Jesus' look at Peter. Because of her background, she had always assumed it was a look of condemnation. She now realized it had to be a look of *undying love*. She wrote,

Peter, I loved you before you were born,
I see you as I created you to be,
knowing your heart will turn back to me,
    the Lamb of God,
who came to die to set you free
from the condemnation that will crucify me.

What kind of look motivates? A look of *undying* love. When disciplining children, what kind of a look do you give them? How does Peter react to this undying and sacrificial love? We learn through Scripture that Peter goes on to be one of Jesus' most devout followers. Today, let's remember the loving look of Jesus.

Saturday: "When I Survey the Wondrous Cross"

Scripture: "May I never boast except in the cross of our Lord Jesus Christ, through which the world has been crucified to me, and I to the world." (Galatians 6:14)

Isaac Watts' goal was to write more joyful hymns. Although the subject of the cross is serious, the hymn moves the singer from contemplation to a joyful commitment to follow after the One who died on that *wondrous* cross.

What are the *vain things* that charm you most but have no everlasting value? What is that *richest gain* that so pales in comparison to the cross?

> Love so amazing, so divine, demands my soul, my life, my all.
>
> "When I Survey the Wondrous Cross" Isaac Watts

"When I Survey the Wondrous Cross"

When I survey the wondrous cross on which the Prince of Glory died,
My richest gain I count but loss, and pour contempt on all my pride.

Forbid it, Lord, that I should boast, save in the cross of Christ, my God:
All the vain things that charm me most, I sacrifice them to his blood.

See, from his head, his hands, his feet, sorrow and love flow mingled down!
Did e'er such love and sorrow meet, or thorns compose so rich a crown?

Were the whole realm of nature mine, that were an offering far too small;
Love so amazing, so divine, demands my soul, my life, my all.

Response: *Lord, I have nothing of material worth to bring You. But I kneel at Your cross and surrender my life to You. Take it all, and use it for Your glory.*

Sunday: "Hosanna, Loud Hosanna!"

Scripture: "Blessed are the peacemakers, for they will be called sons of God." (Matthew 5:9)

Today is Palm Sunday. Let's remember His entry into Jerusalem and find our place in a crowd full of hope and enthusiasm. The hymn "Hosanna, Loud Hosanna!" makes the singer feel a part of the crowd. Can't you just imagine this hymn writer running along with the processional? That is, until you realize that the lyricist was a disabled woman.

Jennette Threlfall wrote this exuberant hymn in the late 1800s. "That ancient song we sing" about Palm Sunday is still as popular and timeless as ever.

Look carefully at the first verse. When do we offer praise that is our best and our simplest? How I would love to see my children blessed by Jesus and closely folded to His breast!

May we ever praise our Redeemer and King!

"Hosanna, Loud Hosanna!"

Hosanna, loud hosanna, the little children sang;
Through pillared court and temple the lovely anthem rang.
To Jesus, Who had blessed them close folded to His breast,
The children sang their praises, the simplest and the best.

From Olivet they followed mid an exultant crowd,
The victor palm branch waving, and chanting clear and loud.
The Lord of men and angels rode on in lowly state,
Nor scorned that little children should on His bidding wait.

"Hosanna in the highest!" that ancient song we sing,
For Christ is our Redeemer, the Lord of heaven our King.
O may we ever praise Him with heart and life and voice,
And in His blissful presence eternally rejoice!

> "Peacemakers who sow in peace raise a harvest of righteousness." (James 3:18)

Response: *Prince of Peace, today we celebrate your entry into Jerusalem. In honor of the peace you longed to bring, we, too, long to be peacemakers. Show us where we've hurt others and help us ask forgiveness. May we forgive those who have hurt us, and seek to bring peace.*

Works Cited

1. Bob Deffinbaugh, Th.M, "The Last Supper (Luke 22:1–23)," http://www.bible.org

2. *Matthew Henry Commentary,* in Accordance Bible software. CD-ROM, version 5.7. Oak Tree Software, Inc.

3. Gariepy, Henry, *40 Days with the Savior: Preparing Your Heart for Easter, Meditations on the Final Days and Suffering of Our Lord* (Nashville: TN: Thomas Nelson, 1995), 40–41.

4. Deffinbaugh, "The Passover Plan: Man Proposes, God Disposes," http://www.bible.org.
——, "The Last Supper (Luke 22:1–23)," http://www.bible.org.

5. Bishop, Jim, *The Day Christ Died: The Inspiring Classic on the Last 24 Hours of Jesus' Life* (San Francisco: Harper, 1957), 7, 18–19.
MacArthur, John, *The Murder of Jesus: A Study of How Jesus Died* (Nashville, TN: Thomas Nelson, 2000), 26.

6. MacArthur, 26.

7. Deffinbaugh, Th.M, "The Passover Plan: Man Proposes, God Disposes," http://www.bible.org.
The MacArthur Study Bible, (Nashville, TN: Thomas Nelson, Word Publishing, 1997), 1571.

8. Deffinbaugh, Th.M, "The Last Supper (Luke 22:1–23)" http://www.bible.org.

9. Ray Vander Laan and Focus on the Family Video (That the World May Know Series), *The True Easter Story, That the World May Know* (Grand Rapids, MI: Zondervan, 2000.

10. http://www.familybible.org/FAQ/Baptism.html
http://www.biblestudymanuals.net/jewish marriage customs.html

11. Lucado, Max, *The Final Week of Jesus* (Multnomah: Multnomah Books, 1994), 94.

12. MacArthur, *The Murder of Jesus: A Study of How Jesus Died,* 47.
Gariepy, 43.

13. Lucado, 92–94.

14. Vander Laan and Focus on the Family Video (That the World May Know Series), *Faith Lessons on the Death and Resurrection of the Messiah: The Weight of the World* (Grand Rapids, MI: Zondervan, 1997, 1998) Volume 4, Video 2.

15. Zugibe, Frederick, *The Cross and the Shroud: A Medical Inquiry into the Crucifixion* (New York: Paragon House, 1988), 3.
Bishop, Jim, *The Day Christ Died: The Inspiring Classic on the Last 24 Hours of Jesus' Life* (San Francisco: Harper, 1957), 169.

16. MacArthur, 69.

17. Ibid., 66–78.

18. Lucado, 93.

19. MacArthur, 94.
Haidle, Helen, *Journey to the Cross: The Complete Easter Story for Young Readers* (Grand Rapids, MI: Zonderkidz, 2001), 93.

20. MacArthur, 110.

21. Ibid., 108.

22. Ibid., 162.

23. Haidle, 94; MacArthur, 104–105, 108.

24. MacArthur, 112.

25. Ibid., 115.

26. Ibid., 136.

Death and Resurrection

Last week we traveled with Jesus from triumphal entry into Jerusalem to tragic abandonment, ending with Jesus' *religious* trials. We will now explore the *political* trials—fast-paced scene changes with increased persecution. Try to experience the loss of Jesus with the same pain as His followers; they do not understand the prophecy about resurrection or know the end of the story. Place bookmarks at John 18, Luke 23, Matthew 27, and Mark 15.

Monday: Arrest, Interrogation, and Persecution— Part II

Read John 18:28–32 (Scene Eight).

Pilate has to come *outside* to address the crowd because the Jews cannot enter the home of a non-Jew or they will defile themselves for Friday's Passover.[1]

Though Jewish leaders considered blasphemy to be a crime punishable by death, the Romans did not. The Jewish death penalty was carried out by stoning, but according to prophecy, Jesus had to be lifted up. Do you see the problem?

Read John 18:33–38 (Scene Eight B).

1. In your own words, write Jesus' responses to Pilate's statements (verses 34, 36, 37).

Pilate's statement:	**Jesus' Answer:**
1. Are you the king of the Jews?	
2. What is it you have done?	
3. You are a king!	
4. What is truth?	

Read Luke 23:5–12 (Scene Nine).

Pilate wants out of the Jesus mess, so he passes Jesus off to Herod, since Jesus is from Herod's political region.

Herod must be shocked when He sees Jesus. MacArthur describes,

How different Christ must have looked from the strong, prophetic miracle worker Herod expected to see! His face was already badly bruised and swollen from the abuse He had taken. Spittle and blood were drying in His matted hair. Tired and physically weakened from a sleepless night, He stood before Herod, bound and under guard like a common criminal.[2]

2. What does Herod hope for in Jesus (verse 8)?

_____

_____

3. Why do you think Jesus answers Pilate but not Herod?

_____

📖 Read Luke 23:13–16 and Mark 15:6–14 (Scene 10).

Pilate still cannot find anything wrong with Jesus, and Pilate's wife even sends a note of warning (Matthew 27:19). Since a prisoner can be set free, Pilate offers to release Jesus. But the crowd prefers Barabbas, an insurrectionist and murderer. The cries of "Crucify him!" intensify. Pilate decides to *punish* Jesus. Maybe this will quench the crowd's cries for blood.

📖 Read Matthew 27:27–30 (Scene 11).

4. These four short verses are packed with details about Christ's torture. List these actions:

Mark 15:19 adds that the soldiers fell on their knees and paid homage to Him; John 19:1 includes that Pilate took Jesus and had him flogged. A flogging can mean death itself. The cat-of-nine tails had nine cords. Attached to the ends of the cords were lead balls, metal, or broken bones that gouged the skin. Jesus' hands are tied to a post. The Jews restricted the flogging to thirty-nine lashes, but the *Romans* had no such rules. Jesus is flogged by *Romans*.[3]

The Cross and the Shroud: A Medical Inquiry into the Crucifixion by Dr. Zugibe delves into the physical toll of flogging.

The bits of metal dug deep into the flesh, ripping small blood vessels, nerves, muscle, and skin. . . . The

Old Testament Prophecy Fulfilled: "See, my servant will act wisely; he will be raised and lifted up and highly exalted." (Isaiah 52:13)

"Just as Moses lifted up the snake in the desert, so the Son of Man must be lifted up." (John 3:14)

victim writhed and twisted in agony, falling to his knees, only to be jerked back on his feet time and time again until he could no longer stand up. Bouts of vomiting, tremors, seizures, and fainting fits occurred at varying intervals. . . . The victim was reduced to an exhausted, mangled mass of flesh with a craving for water. He was in a state of traumatic shock.[4]

Some believe the naked victim was shackled to a low column and bent over.[5] Others claim it involved a post and the wrists tied high, the body almost off the ground. If kidneys or certain arteries were wounded, the victim could die.[6] A flogging could expose veins, muscles, and sinews from the tops of the shoulders all the way to the backs of the legs[7] and because of the hematidrosis experienced in the Garden of Gethsemane, Jesus' skin would be extremely sensitive.[8]

The crown of thorns had two-inch long barbs.[9] Because of the sensitivity of the nerves, and the vascular nature of the scalp, Jesus experiences a spiking pain and much bleeding.[10] Dr. Zugibe writes,

> They paid homage to the new king as they filed past, kneeling and then striking him across the face with the scepter and spitting on him. His cheeks and nose became reddened, bruised, and swollen, and stabbing pains that felt like electric shocks or red-hot pokers traversed his face, immobilizing him so he was afraid to turn lest the pain might reoccur. His face became distorted, and Jesus tensed his whole body so that he would not move, for every movement activated little trigger zones, bringing on agonizing attacks.[11]

During the flogging scene in Mel Gibson's *The Passion of the Christ,* I buried my head and plugged my ears. Later when I acted the part of Mary Magdalene in our local passion play, I recalled the movie scenes and uttered the words I had longed to scream, "STOP IT! STOP IT! STOP IT!"

Old Testament Prophecy Fulfilled: "I offered my back to those who beat me, my cheeks to those who pulled out my beard; I did not hide my face from mocking and spitting." (Isaiah 50:6)

Mosaic Law
". . . but he must not give him more than forty lashes. If he is flogged more than that, your brother will be degraded in your eyes." (Deuteronomy 25:3)

But *should* we stop remembering what Jesus did for us? My friend Barbara asked her teenage daughter, "Do you remember how young you were when you fully understood the story of Jesus' crucifixion?"

Hannah said she couldn't remember a time when she *didn't* know. She even recalled how sad she felt as a toddler hearing about Jesus being beaten and hung on a cross. *But* she thought she would never have been such a joyful and confident little girl had she not known that God loved her *that* much and that her friend Jesus had *that kind* of power. Hannah wisely concluded, "Until you experience the sadness of Christ's rejection and crucifixion by his own people, you just can't experience all the joy, excitement, and power of the resurrection."

> **Old Testament Prophecy Fulfilled:** "Just as there were many who were appalled at him—his appearance was so disfigured beyond that of any man and his form marred beyond human likeness." (Isaiah 52:14)

Let's consider this from Jesus' followers' point of view. Remember, they do not grasp the potential of the resurrection.

📖 Read John 19:4–17 (Scene 12).

Pilate reveals a bloodied and beaten man, hoping to appease the crowd. When you see Him, do you long to sing?

O Sacred Head, now wounded, with grief and shame weighed down,
Now scornfully surrounded with thorns Thy only crown;
How art Thou pale with anguish, with sore abuse and scorn!

5. Look at John 19:10–11 and record Pilate's three questions and Jesus' responses:

Pilate's question: **Jesus' Response:**
1.
2.
3.

The presentation of a beaten Jesus wearing a crown of thorns and purple robe is not enough. The crowd yells, "Crucify! Crucify!" How did we get from "Hosanna!" to "Crucify Him?" Some of those in the crowd may be the same Palm Sunday individuals now disappointed that Jesus is not the leader they wanted. Or maybe they've been provoked by the overwhelming number of priests and police dominating the crowd. Or perhaps since it's still early Friday morning, some of Jesus' followers may not even know He's been arrested.[12]

After Pilate presents Jesus, he tries to wash his hands of all guilt. The crowd is willing to take on the consequences of their actions. Barabbas is released, and Jesus is led out. The soldiers mock Jesus and rip off the purple robe, which no doubt has stuck to His raw flesh. They return Jesus' clothes and lay a heavy cross on Him (Matthew 27:31).

📖 Read Luke 23:26–31, Mark 15:21–22 (Scene 13).

Jesus stumbles his way to Golgotha (skull), a public hanging site, carrying His own patibulum or crossbeam (or perhaps even a full cross), which could weigh anywhere from 30 to 110 pounds. He also may have worn a sign around His neck identifying His crime, much the same way the Passover lambs were marked as belonging to a certain family.[13] Combining the titles from the gospels resulted in this label written in Greek, Latin, and Hebrew and posted above Jesus' head at Golgotha.[14]

THIS IS JESUS OF NAZARETH, THE KING OF THE JEWS

Simon of Cyrene is ordered to carry the cross. Can you imagine if *you* were ordered to carry Christ's cross? One year in the passion play we lacked a Simon of Cyrene. This turned out to be providential, because someone suggested that one of our Roman soldiers actually grab a spectator from the crowd. This spectator in street clothes forced all of us to consider what it was like to carry Jesus' cross.

What about the women? Though it was dangerous to be associated with a condemned man, they follow, even crying publicly. Jesus stops for a moment and addresses their tears (Luke 23:28–30). He prophesies terrible times for Jerusalem's future by quoting Old Testament prophecy (Hosea 10:8). (Indeed in AD 70 the temple is left in ruins by the Romans, and the Jews slaughtered.[15] According to historian Josephus Titus, there are so many crucifixions taking place after this Roman conquest; there is a shortage of wood as well as places to set up the crosses.[16])

> **Old Testament Prophecy Fulfilled:** "He was oppressed and afflicted, yet he did not open his mouth; he was led like a lamb to the slaughter, and as a sheep before her shearers is silent, so he did not open his mouth." (Isaiah 53:7)

The women are there on the Way of Sorrow. They don't know what is happening except that everything is terribly frightening, and they are about to lose the person they love most. Jesus released them from the burden of demons, illnesses, and religious persecution, and they thought His Lordship would continue. Now it appears He will die on the cross. He is about to give up everything for them, but they have no idea what it will mean for their earthly and heavenly futures. They do not anticipate His resurrection.

Jesus' Words in Action: When my friend Kelly learned her neighbor's baby needed a new liver, she decided to donate a piece of her own to help save him. When she risked her own life for Michael's, she invested deeply. She paid a price so that he might live. Now Michael is not just an ordinary little boy to her.

How much more did Jesus sacrifice for *you*? How much more does He want *you* to have life eternal? You need to understand the value of Christ's sacrifice and that His grace was purchased at a great price.

Tuesday: The Cross and Christ's Death
Seven Last Words

Like the women standing beneath the cross, today we will fix our eyes on Jesus. Jesus said very little while hanging from the cross. Today we will *hear* Him utter His seven last phrases and *see* Him endure the cross so that we can celebrate His victory when He sits at the right hand of the throne of God.

Each Gospel records at least twenty verses on the death of Christ. Each writer highlights certain portions of that final day. In today's study we'll flip back and forth. Place bookmarks in the following four locations to simplify your study: Matthew 27:33, Mark 15:22, Luke 23:32, and John 19:17. These last few hours of Jesus' life teach many valuable lessons, but today's study will be heavy and demand more time.

> "Let us fix our eyes on Jesus, the author and perfecter of our faith, who for the joy set before him endured the cross, scorning its shame, and sat down at the right hand of the throne of God."
> (Hebrews 12:2)

Timeline—The Clock ticks down . . . (Third hour) 9:00 a.m. until noon:

📖 Read Mark 15:23–28, Luke 23:32–34, and John 19:19–24.

The place of crucifixion was probably near Jerusalem's North Wall (see map on p. 83) by a gate on a busy street so all would know His "crime."[17] When Jesus arrives at Golgotha, the soldiers tear off Jesus' clothes, which have become encrusted to His bleeding back.[18] Though we usually see pictures of Him in a loincloth, it is more likely He was stripped to nakedness.[19]

1. What do we know about the specific crime of the other two men crucified with Christ (Mark 15:27)?

_____

_____

2. What was Jesus offered to drink? Why do you think He abstained (Mark 15:23)?

_____

_____

A mixture of vinegar and gall (a bitter myrrh narcotic) is offered to help numb the pain. Jesus does not receive it. He wants to be fully alert to everything that happens.[20] Thus, when a seven-inch nail, much like a railroad spike, is driven into either the palm of His hand in the fold near His thumb[21] or in His wrists, smashing His median nerve, he experiences a terrible burning pain.[22]

> **Old Testament Prophecy Fulfilled:** "Dogs have surrounded me; a band of evil men has encircled me, they have pierced my hands and my feet." (Psalm 22:16)

The cross is raised, causing the weight of His body to suddenly shift downwards, pulling his shoulders out of joint. Over time, fluid will accumulate in his lungs and heart.[23]

Old Testament Prophecy Fulfilled: "I am poured out like water, and all my bones are out of joint. My heart has turned to wax; it has melted away within me." (Psalm 22:14)

Though the Bible focuses more on the pain of Christ's crucifixion in the *Old* Testament rather than in the *New*, we now know much from research and reenactments. Jesus' mangled and scourged flesh scrapes against the rough wood of the cross; His muscles cramp; He feels the tremendous drag on his shoulder muscles and the unrelenting pain of His nail-pierced hands and feet. Sharp pains shoot through His thorn-imbedded scalp. Dehydrated, He experiences an unquenchable thirst. He becomes nauseous and feverish. Jesus has been deprived of sleep, food, and water for quite some time.[24] And, oh, how He longs for the companionship of His Father.

In medical terms, He experiences hypovolemic shock (great blood loss), respiratory acidosis (acidic blood leading to irregular heartbeat), pericardial effusion (fluid around the heart), and pleural effusion (fluid on the lungs). The heart goes into overdrive; His blood pressure drops; kidneys fail, and He becomes thirsty from the loss of blood.[25] And yet, in the midst of that pain, He prays for his persecutors: "Father, forgive them, for they do not know what they are doing" (Luke 23:34).

> "Love your enemies and pray for those who persecute you, that you may be sons of your Father in heaven." (Matthew 5:44)

3. We see Jesus live out His earlier words, "For if you forgive men when they sin against you, your heavenly Father will also forgive you" (Matthew 6:14). Given Jesus' witness and the way He forgives, is there any reason we *cannot* forgive? Is there someone you need to forgive today?

_____

4. The sign over Jesus is written in Aramaic (a Semitic language with many similarities to Hebrew), Latin, and Greek. What is the conflict over the wording (John 19:19–22)? To this day, what is the difference between *saying* who Jesus is and just repeating who *others* say He is?

_____

_____

> "If someone strikes you on one cheek, turn to him the other also. If someone takes your cloak, do not stop him from taking your tunic" (Luke 6:29).

Jesus may own five pieces of clothing: sandals, robe, headpiece, belt and tunic. If a *quaternion* (squad of four) guards him, they'd each have one piece and need to gamble for the seamless tunic.[26] The soldiers cast lots, fulfilling the Old Testament prophecy, "They divide my garments among them and cast lots for my clothing" (Psalm 22:18).

As if the physical pain is not enough, Jesus is mocked. Soldiers, spectators and even the criminals taunt Him. Once again, Old Testament prophecy is fulfilled.

5. Read Matthew 27:39–44 and Luke 23:35–37. Then list the insults hurled at Christ.

6. In your Bible, circle the titles that are incorrect. If they are *correct*, what is the problem?

_____

Old Testament Prophecy Fulfilled: "But I am a worm and not a man, scorned by men and despised by the people. All who see me mock me; they hurl insults, shaking their heads." (Psalm 22:6–7)

Many know the *name* of Jesus, and even demons call Him *Lord,* but it doesn't mean they give Him glory. What about us? Do we ascribe to Him the glory due His name?

Jesus is crucified with criminals, one on each side. As the hours progress, each man makes a choice about the Son of Man. Just like today, each of us has a choice of whether to follow Jesus or not.

7. Read Luke 23:39–43. In your own words rewrite the dialogue from Luke 23:39–43 as if it were a script.

CRIMINAL:
CRIMINAL: (*to other criminal*)
CRIMINAL: (*to Jesus*)
JESUS:

Old Testament Prophecy Fulfilled: "For he bore the sin of many, and made intercession for the transgressors." (Isaiah 53:12)

One woman responded to this question by saying that one criminal said, *"Get me down!"* while the other said, *"Take me up!"*

Jesus knows the heart of the criminal beside him. It matters not that the criminal has not been baptized, lived a sinless life, or spent a day in the synagogue. The man believes. Jesus came to die a criminal's death between criminals so that this man—and all else who believe—might have eternal life.

"I tell you the truth, whoever hears my word and believes him who sent me has eternal life and will not be condemned; he has crossed over from death to life." (John 5:24)

Jesus spoke few words on the cross, but His words to the thief must have brought great assurance:

"I tell you the truth, today you will be with me in paradise" (Luke 23:43).

I would love to hear those words on my deathbed. I would love to hear the voice of Jesus confirm that I will spend eternity with Him in a place far better than earth. Can you say today with assurance that one day you will join Jesus in heaven?

📖 Read John 19:25–27.

Jesus' mother, his mother's sister, Mary the wife of Clopas, and Mary Magdalene stand near the cross and witness this degrading scene where their Lord is treated as a criminal and hung naked before the masses. Jesus stops to recognize the pain of His mother: " 'Dear woman, here is your son,' and to the disciple, 'Here is your mother' " (John 19:26–27).

8. How does Jesus look out for both John and Mary? Why does He select *John* to be a son to His mother?

_____

_____

If John then took Mary away from the cross, that left Mary's sister, Mary the wife of Clopas, and Mary Magdalene. *Always Mary Magdalene.* As these women mourn for an enemy of Rome, they take a risk, especially by nearing the cross. These women could endure the same crucifixion for their loyalty.[27] How long could *you* stand below the cross under those circumstances?

According to Matthew it is the sixth hour (using the Jewish system), or *noon* our time.[28] From the sixth until the ninth hour, the sky turns black. And at 3:00 p.m., Jesus cries out, " 'Eloi, Eloi, lama sabachthani?' which means, 'My God, my God, why have you forsaken me?' " (Matthew 27:46). endure the same crucifixion for their loyalty.[28] How long could *you* stand below the cross under those circumstances?

Noon until 3:00 p.m.

📖 Read Matthew 27:45–50 and John 19:28–30.

Those standing near think he is crying out for Elijah to save Him, when in fact Jesus is quoting the words from Psalm 22:1, "My God, my God, why have you forsaken me? Why are you so far from saving me, so far from the words of my groaning?" But Jesus doesn't need salvation. He would choose death even if He had to hammer Himself to the cross and hang one-handed.

Jesus has had no water for eighteen hours. An exhausting evening of prayer in the garden was followed by sweating due to the pain of scourging and the crown of thorns, plus hauling the heavy cross; He has lost much water.[29] John 19:28 comments, "Later, knowing that all was now completed, and so that the Scripture would be fulfilled, Jesus said, 'I am thirsty.' "

Old Testament Prophecy Fulfilled: "My strength is dried up like a potsherd, and my tongue sticks to the roof of my mouth; you lay me in the dust of death" (Psalm 22:15).

9. What is the dying man on the cross offered to drink (see Matthew 27:48; John 19:29)?

_____

_____

> "Greater love has no one than this, that he lay down his life for his friends." (John 15:13)
>
>

The second liquid offered is a cheap, sour wine used to make the victim's life linger in extended pain.[30] According to John, what do they use to put this liquid to Jesus' lips? A hyssop plant. Do you remember what was used to spread the blood around the doorframe on the night of Passover? Hyssop.[31]

Old Testament Prophecy Fulfilled: "Scorn has broken my heart and has left me helpless; I looked for sympathy, but there was none, for comforters, but I found none. They put gall in my food and gave me vinegar for my thirst." (Psalm 69:20–21)

We are now down to Jesus' near-final three triumphant words. John 19:30 relates, "When he had received the drink, Jesus said, **'It is finished.'** With that, he bowed his head and gave up his spirit" (emphasis added).

He knows that His mission on earth is nearly completed, He has reached the finish line, and His love is greater than the pain. With every last ounce of strength, Jesus calls out in a loud voice, " 'Father, into your hands I commit my spirit.' When he had said this, he breathed his last" (Luke 23:46).

The shofar is blown at 3 p.m., announcing the sacrifice of the lamb.[32]

10. Read Matthew 27:51–53. Prior to Jesus' death, the spectators experienced darkness during the day. What other miraculous events do they witness?

_____

_____

Once a year, on the Day of Atonement, the high priest entered the Holy of Holies to offer the blood of a sacrifice behind a 19 x 60 foot veil, perhaps six inches thick.[33]

11. Who tears the temple curtain in half? Why does it need tearing?

_____

_____

The answer to that question can be found in Hebrews 10:19–22, which explains Old Testament practices and how they impact the New Testament! What a privilege we now have to come straight to God in prayer!

> *Therefore, brothers, since we have confidence to enter the Most Holy Place by the blood of Jesus, by a new and living way opened for us through the curtain, that is, his body, and since we have a great priest over the house of God, let us draw near to God with a sincere heart in full assurance of faith, having our hearts sprinkled to cleanse us from a guilty conscience and having our bodies washed with pure water. (Hebrews 10:19–22)*

The old system of sacrifices is over, torn away. Now all can freely approach God.[34]

12. How do onlookers react to the strange happenings (see Matthew 27:54; Luke 23:47–49)?

_____

_____

There is a huge "BUT" in Luke 23:47–49. In contrast to the other observers, what do the women do? They stand and watch. What is going through their minds? Mark 15:40–41 reminds us which women remain at the cross: women who followed Him and cared for His needs in Galilee and others who came with Him to Jerusalem and follow Him to the end.

📖 Read John 19:31–37.

It is now Friday afternoon. The hours are counting down until the Sabbath. According to the Old Testament, Jesus' body must be taken off the cross (see Deuteronomy 21:23).

One way to speed someone's death during crucifixion is to break his legs. This either causes the victim to be unable to push his body upwards to gasp for air,[35] or deals the "final blow" resulting in deep shock, coma, and death.[36] After the soldiers take a mallet to the other two men's legs, they discover Jesus is already dead. To prove the death, a soldier pierces Jesus' side, releasing blood and water.

Prophetic Old Testament scripture continues to be fulfilled, detail by detail:

"*. . . he protects all his bones, not one of them will be broken*" (Psalm 34:20)

"*. . . he was pierced for our transgressions*" (Isaiah 53:5a)

Jesus' Words in Action: Max Lucado writes, "*The very instrument of the cross is symbolic, the vertical beam of holiness intersecting with the horizontal bar of love.*"[37] Draw a picture of Lucado's words and place yourself beside the cross, write a prayer to Jesus, or in some way put Jesus' actions into words or a picture.

Wednesday: Waiting and Wondering

Think back to a time when you experienced a sudden and shocking loss. What happens *after* you learn of such tragedies? Quite often you enter a period of waiting. You feel numb; you sob; you can't sleep, and when you finally are able to sleep, it is interrupted, fitful sleep. You awaken to a vague and growing, gut-wrenching sorrow as you remember your loss. What do you do when your beloved is in the grave and you have no one to turn to, and home is no longer home? Do you hang onto your memories because you can't fathom a lonely future without your beloved?

Jesus' female followers have just watched their Lord, friend, and savior die a horrible death on a cross. The man who changed their lives is now dead, His body sealed in a tomb. They need to return to the grave because they have nowhere else to go and they need to be near Him. These women bring anointing oils. Perhaps the fragrance is on their hands. Perhaps the words from the cross linger in their thoughts. Sorrowful images must play in their minds. How can they make sense of it all?

As we consider their grief, let's try to make a little sense of what *they* see and hear by comparing it to what we observe in Old Testament prophecy.

His face. . . . I can barely look at Him or even recognize Him.
What pain and suffering He endured.

I offered my back to those who beat me, my cheeks to those who pulled out my beard; I did not hide my face from mocking and spitting. (Isaiah 50:6)

Why did they despise Him so? He was a healer, a teacher, and a friend! I loved Him so!

He was despised and rejected by men, a man of sorrows, and familiar with suffering. Like one from whom men hide their faces he was despised, and we esteemed him not. (Isaiah 53:3)

At times Jesus didn't even speak up. Not a single word!
He wouldn't defend Himself? Why did He suffer silently?

He was oppressed and afflicted, yet he did not open his mouth; he was led like a lamb to the slaughter, and as a sheep before her shearers is silent, so he did not open his mouth. (Isaiah 53:7)

They didn't break His bones but they pierced His side.
It was then that I knew Jesus was dead and it was really all over.

They will look on me, the one they have pierced, and they will mourn for him as one mourns for an only child, and grieve bitterly for him as one grieves for a firstborn son. (Zechariah 12:10)

Now what, O God? What do I do with these feelings of loss?
What do I do with the hope that has died?
I grieve bitterly. How will I heal?

But he was pierced for our transgressions, he was crushed for our iniquities; the punishment that brought us peace was upon him, and by his wounds we are healed. (Isaiah 53:5)

I cried out while Jesus hung on that cross.
I could not understand what was being accomplished.
My Jesus cried out, too.
Did Jesus understand what was happening to Him?

"This grace was given us in Christ Jesus before the beginning of time, but it has now been revealed through the appearing of our Savior, Christ Jesus, who has destroyed death and has brought life and immortality to light through the gospel." (2 Timothy 1:9b–10)

Yet it was the LORD's will to crush him and cause him to suffer, and though the LORD makes his life a guilt offering, he will see his offspring and prolong his days, and the will of the LORD will prosper in his hand. After the suffering of his soul, he will see the light [of life] and be satisfied; by his knowledge my righteous servant will justify many, and he will bear their iniquities. (Isaiah 53:10–11)

📖 Read Psalm 22; Isaiah 52:13–15; 53:1–12 to see what God planned before creation.

Jesus' Words in Action: Do you better understand the planning that went on before creation to ensure that you had the privilege of spending eternity with Him? God loved you so much He would die for you. Beloved, be *loved*. Feel and cherish His great love for you. Your sins were nailed to the cross and paid in full.

> *When you were dead in your sins and in the uncircumcision of your sinful nature, God made you alive with Christ. He forgave us all our sins, having canceled the written code, with its regulations, that was against us and that stood opposed to us; he took it away, nailing it to the cross. (Colossians 2:13–14)*

Thursday: Journey to the Tomb

Today we celebrate Maundy Thursday, when Jesus gave the disciples the commandment to love one another. Yet where are these disciples now? What do you suppose Jesus' followers are asking or secretly wondering? *Is this it? Is Jesus gone forever? What do we do now?* The disciples cower; the women wait, and the rulers worry.

📖 Read Matthew 27:57–66 (also Mark 15:42–47; Luke 23:50–56; John 19:38–42).

Today's reading introduces Joseph of Arimathea. Mark 15:43 provides further information: "Joseph of Arimathea, a prominent member of the Council, who was himself waiting for the kingdom of God, went boldly to Pilate and asked for Jesus' body." Luke 23:51 states that Joseph was good and upright and did not vote for Jesus' execution.

> **Old Testament Prophecy Fulfilled:** "He was assigned a grave with the wicked, and with the rich in his death, though he had done no violence, nor was any deceit in his mouth." (Isaiah 53:9)

1. List what we know about Joseph from Matthew 27:57, 60; Mark 15:43 and Luke 23:51.

_____

_____

John tells us that Joseph was a secret disciple of Jesus because he feared the Jews (John 19:38b). However, there's nothing secretive now. Joseph goes **boldly** to Pilate and asks for Jesus' body. This, too, fulfills prophecy.

Mark informs us Pilate is surprised Jesus is already dead. Pilate summons the centurion and asks if Jesus is dead. After the centurion confirms this, Pilate surrenders the body to Joseph (Mark 15:44–45). Do we need any more proof that Jesus is _dead_?

But brave Joseph does not act alone. John 19:39 records, "He was accompanied by Nicodemus, the man who earlier had visited Jesus at night." Nicodemus? You ask. That name rings a bell. Indeed. Nicodemus is the cowardly Pharisee who came under the cover of darkness to ask Jesus the most important question of Nicodemus' life. Today we're going to go back, and _way_ back, to learn more about Jesus' teachings about eternal life.

📖 Read John 3:1–21.

2. Who is Nicodemus, and to what group does he belong? Why do you think he meets Jesus at night (verse 1)?

_____

_____

Jesus' claims are bolder than Nicodemus' statement. Here is where we get that phrase "born again" (John 3:3). Nicodemus was confused. He's a literalist and asks, "How can a man be born when he is old? . . . Surely he cannot enter a second time into his mother's womb to be born!" (John 3:4).

3. According to Jesus, what must we be born of to enter God's kingdom (verse 5)?

_____

Jesus compares the Holy Spirit to the wind. When Nicodemus persists in questioning, Jesus reminds Him, "You are Israel's teacher and do you not understand these things?" (John 3:10). In John 3 we find some of Jesus' most profound words about His mission being explained to a Pharisee, a member of the Sanhedrin.

4. List what Nicodemus learned about salvation from the following verses.

John 3:13   Son of Man came from heaven
John 3:14–15   Son of Man must be lifted up to bring
                   eternal life.

John 3:16
John 3:17
John 3:18
John 3:19
John 3:20
John 3:21

What is this stuff about Moses lifting up a snake in the desert doing right smack before the big John 3:16? Now we'll have to go *way* back to a few verses from the Old Testament.

While Moses and the Israelites were in the desert, the people whined about their conditions, so the Lord punished them by sending venomous snakes that bit and killed them. The people acknowledged their sin and asked Moses to pray the snakes away (see Numbers 21:5–7). The salvation for the people came in the form of a snake lifted up on a pole. Looking at the snake brought life.

> "Just as Moses lifted up the snake in the desert, so the Son of Man must be lifted up, that everyone who believes in him may have eternal life." (John 3:14–15)

> *The LORD said to Moses, "Make a snake and put it up on a pole; anyone who is bitten can look at it and live." So Moses made a bronze snake and put it up on a pole. Then when anyone was bitten by a snake and looked at the bronze snake, he lived. (Numbers 21:8–9)*

That is what Nicodemus learns in his secret nighttime visit. Now he has come before night, bringing seventy-five pounds of myrrh and aloes to anoint the body of a crucified criminal. He and Joseph wrap the body in strips of clean linen cloth and spices according to Jewish burial customs (John 19:39b–40). The burial cloth is wrapped from Jesus' neck to his feet and then back up the front to His chest. Smaller strips follow.[38]

They place the body in Joseph's new tomb cut out of rock, which is believed by many to be located in the garden where Jesus was crucified (John 19:41). An ordinary person would be laid in the ground, not entombed in stone; this new tomb would have cost thousands of dollars in American money.[39]

Mary Magdalene and the other Mary have left the cross and followed Joseph and Nicodemus all the way to the tomb. Luke records,

> *The women who had come with Jesus from Galilee followed Joseph and saw the tomb and how his body was laid in it. Then they went home and prepared spices and perfumes. But they rested on the Sabbath in obedience to the commandment. (Luke 23:55–56)*

5. Although Jesus' disciples may not be thinking about the three days, the Jewish leaders are. On the day after Preparation Day, the chief priests and the Pharisees go to see Pilate. What do they remember that Jesus prophesied, and what is their concern (Matthew 27:62–64)?

_____

_____

A cord is strung across the tombstone and glued down with wax or clay. The official seal of a "signet ring" is imprinted on the wax.[40] A squad (4–16 men) stands guard at the tomb.[41] A broken seal or opened grave meant death to the soldiers.[42] What would you be thinking? *Now what do we do?*

Jesus' Words in Action: One of the most telling statements Jesus made to Nicodemus is recorded in John 3:16, the verse many of us memorize in our childhood. Nicodemus knew God loved Him so much he could come out of the darkness and into the light and have a relationship with His Savior. Indeed Nicodemus must have believed, for when the disciples failed their Savior, he joined Joseph to anoint Christ's body.

What does John 3:16 really mean to you? Look at it with new eyes and see that Jesus is the One lifted up and ready to heal, forgive, and bring eternal life.

Put your name in the verse today: "For God so loved _____ that he gave _____ his one and only Son, that if _____ believes in him _____ shall not perish but have eternal life."

Good Friday: "O Sacred Head"

Today is Good Friday, and we will take a break from our study. Consider what Jesus did for you and how dark the world would be without His light.

Scripture: "He was despised and rejected by men, a man of sorrows, and familiar with suffering. Like one from whom men hide their faces he was despised, and we esteemed him not." (Isaiah 53:3)

📖 Read the verses of this song, written in a minor key, and picture Jesus' sacrifice for your salvation.

> Lord, let me never, never outlive my love to Thee!
>
> "O Sacred Head" by Hans Leo Hassler

"O Sacred Head"

O Sacred Head, now wounded, with grief and
    shame weighed down,
Now scornfully surrounded with thorns Thy only
    crown;
How art Thou pale with anguish, with sore abuse
    and scorn!
How does that visage languish which once was
    bright as morn!

What Thou, my Lord, hast suffered was all for sin-
    ners' gain:
Mine, mine was the transgression, but Thine the
    deadly pain.
Lo, here I fall, my Savior! 'Tis I deserve Thy place;
Look on me with Thy favor; vouch-safe to me Thy grace.

What language shall I borrow to thank Thee, dearest Friend,
For this Thy dying sorrow, Thy pity without end?
O make me Thine forever! And, should I fainting be,
Lord, let me never, never outlive my love to Thee!

> "He is not here; he has risen! Remember how he told you, while he was still with you in Galilee: 'The Son of Man must be delivered into the hands of sinful men, be crucified and on the third day be raised again.' "(Luke 24:6–7)

"O Sacred Head" by Hans Leo Hassler is part of a longer poem depicting the many parts of Jesus' body that suffered during the Passion. Though we focus on the head, Jesus endured great pain in His face, heart, breast, side, hands, knees, and feet. He did this for you and me. No language can express our thankfulness except perhaps the language of love.

Response: *O Lord, today is Good Friday, and yet nothing about it was good for you. You endured great torment and* *anguish. But because of your great love for me, you remained on the cross so my sins would be forgiven. It was my transgression; I deserved to be on the cross. What words can I say to you, my dear Friend? I can say, "I love You," and "Thank You." I long to spend eternity with you.*

The Great Vigil Saturday: Christ Arose

On Easter 1874, hymn writer Robert Lowry was especially touched by Luke 24:6–7 and wrote the hymn "Christ Arose."[43] The morning after the Sabbath went from a somber, emotional low to a beautiful high, and Lowry's hymn does the same. The verses are slow and mournful, but the chorus is celebratory with a trumpet-like melody announcing, "Good news!" The piece seems to move from Saturday's grief to Sunday's joy.

My cousin Joan first heard this hymn sung by her two-year-old daughter Lena, but the words didn't quite make sense so she asked Lena about them. "Daddy taught me the song," Lena explained, belting out another chorus of "UP from the GRAVY a ROSE!" After Lena's daddy translated the words correctly, Joan understood the deeper significance of the hymn. But perhaps her toddler's version is also powerfully descriptive!

> "When the Sabbath was over, Mary Magdalene, Mary the mother of James, and Salome bought spices so that they might go to anoint Jesus' body." (Mark 16:1)
>
>

"Christ Arose"

Verse 1
Low in the grave He lay, Jesus, my Savior!
Waiting the coming day, Jesus, my Lord!

Verse 2
Vainly they watched His bed, Jesus my Savior!
Vainly they sealed the dead, Jesus my Lord!

Chorus:
Up from the grave He arose
With a mighty triumph o'er His foes
He arose a victor from the dark domain
And He lives forever with His saints to reign;
He arose! He arose! Hallelujah! Christ arose!

Today is the Great Vigil. Though we have a sense of great anticipation for Resurrection Sunday, remember that Jesus' followers felt great sorrow and loss and didn't anticipate the "happily ever after" Easter ending.

We don't read Jesus' followers counting down "Day 3, Day 2, Day 1. Ready, Set, GO FIND HIM!" I can't imagine the disciples asking Peter, "Hey Peter! Do you remember *exactly* what Jesus said about His death? Never mind, you didn't even listen to that part about the rooster."

"Matthew, just what did He say again?"

No, the only people even checking the tomb are the *unbelievers* worried the body will be *stolen* and the women who want to anoint the **dead** body. We see no resurrection hope or resurrection joy.

Put your bookmarks at Matthew 28, Mark 16, Luke 24, and John 20. We'll flip back and forth as we look at four accounts of resurrection Sunday.

The chronology of these passages is sometimes confusing. This only reinforces the accuracy of the story. Historian Paul Maier writes, "And the fact that differences among them were not edited out or harmonized shows both the honesty of Early Church copyists and the fact that there was no agreed upon— and therefore partially fabricated—version."[44]

But rather than focusing on the harmonization of the gospels, let's focus on various aspects of that glorious morning. Today's study begins the day *after* the Sabbath. At some point the women purchase spices and go to the tomb. Boy, are they in for a surprise!

📖 Read Matthew 28:1–7 and Mark 16:1–8.

1. What words describe the angel?

_____

2. What is the reaction of the guards?

_____

3. Why do you think the women experience such fear?

_____

Thirty-three years before, around the time of Jesus' birth, angels also frightened Mary, Zechariah, and the shepherds in the fields. Seemingly, angels always need to say, "Do not be afraid." Similarly, just as the angel instructed the shepherds at Jesus' birth to go see baby Jesus, the angels instruct the women at Jesus' death to "Come and see the place where he lay"

(Matthew 28:5–6). But this time Jesus is not in swaddling clothes; He has vanished and left behind the strips of cloth.

4. The angel gives the women instructions. What are they (Matthew 28:7; Mark 16:7)?

_____

_____

These women are the *first* to hear the Good News. The angel says, "HE HAS RISEN!" The words they are to announce make them the first missionaries to tell the resurrection story. And yet, when they leave, they leave with mixed emotions.

5. What do Matthew 28:8 and Mark 16:8 say about the women's reactions?

_____

_____

📖 Read Luke 24:1–8 for a third description of Resurrection morning.

6. How do the women react to two men wearing clothes that gleam like lightning?

_____

_____

In AD 30, female witnesses are not admissible in court, suggesting that in a world where women are second-class citizens, men do not trust women to provide reliable information. What will happen when they testify about what they've seen?

_____

_____

📖 Read John 20:2–10.

7. Who do the women tell first, and what is the reaction?

_____

_____

8. Describe the placement of the burial cloths (verse 7)?

_____

The headpiece is folded, the strips of cloth just lying there. Paul Maier writes, "According to this literal interpretation of the Greek, in which John was written, it seemed as if the body simply vanished from its grave wrappings, leaving them exactly in place except for gravity flattening the main shroud."[45]

Though John 20:8 records that they believe, verse 9 adds an intriguing parenthetical note: (They still do not understand that Jesus had to rise from the dead.)

9. What exactly *do* the disciples believe? What do *you* believe?

_____

_____

Jesus' Words in Action: A week before Easter, I took my daughters to see their adopted Grandma, Aunt Rae, who was dying of cancer. The girls and I had longed to say "goodbye" but had been prevented from visiting because of our various illnesses. When we finally arrived at the nursing home for our final visit, Aunt Rae had just slipped into a deep sleep or coma. Nine-year-old Christine pulled out her violin and began playing a chorus by Handel as we all watched for any flicker of awareness.

When Christine finished, Christine turned back to us, and I saw tears streaming down her face. Christine had quietly sobbed while she played. My heart broke for her and for my seven-year-old daughter, Julia, who longed to say "I love you" once again.

But because of Easter, someday they will.

On the way home, we talked about how we would see Aunt Rae and talk to her again. She died before Easter and would spend a glorious resurrection day in heaven. We may not always get to say all our earthly goodbyes, but we look forward to an eternity of hellos.

Paul Maier describes Easter as the only holiday that looks backwards as well as forwards in history. It's a festival that both recognizes the Passion and celebrates a future of glorious reunions.[46] Similarly, Philip Yancey echoes that Jesus' scars give him hope.

> Because of Easter, I can hope that the tears we shed, the blows we receive, the emotional pain, the heartache over lost friends and loved ones, all these will become memories, like Jesus' scars. Scars never completely go away, but neither do they hurt any longer.

We will have re-created bodies, a re-created heaven and earth. We will have a new start, an Easter start.[47]

What gives you hope? What gives you a new Easter start?

That which can seem so dead can be made alive with His resurrection power. The One who conquered death can bring life to a stale church, reconciliation to fractured relationships, and resurrected love to stale marriages.

In *The Power of a Praying Wife*, Stormie Omartian highlights Mary Magdalene's joy in discovering Jesus' resurrection.

> The joy of seeing something hopelessly dead brought to life is the greatest joy we can know. The power that resurrected Jesus is the very same power that will resurrect the dead places of your marriage and put life back into it. "God both raised up the Lord and will also raise us up by His power." (1 Corinthians 6:14)[48]

What seems dead in your life? What needs healing or reconciliation? Bring it to the Lord in consistent and committed prayer. Have an Easter heart full of hope.

Sunday: "Christ, the Lord, Is Risen Today"

On Resurrection Sunday, I used to pick up my toddler and dance around singing the "Easter Song." One of my new favorites is Travis Cottrell's "Alive, Forever, Amen!" If you don't have a great Easter praise song to blast in your house on Easter morning, quite frankly, you need one.

> Love's redeeming work is done, Alleluia!
>
> *"Christ the Lord is Risen Today" by Charles Wesley*

"Christ the Lord Is Risen Today" by Charles Wesley is the Easter equivalent to "Angels We Have Heard on High" with its melismatic 10-note "Alleluia" ending the phrases. Today in church, remember Easter is not about stained glass windows, getting a new dress and hat, and planting tulips and lilies. Instead it's about new life in Christ! Sing out loudly and with great joy! Celebrate with someone!

"Christ, the Lord, Is Risen Today"

Christ, the Lord, is risen today, Alleluia!
Sons of men and angels say, Alleluia!

Raise your joys and triumphs high, Alleluia!
Sing, ye heavens, and earth, reply, Alleluia!

Love's redeeming work is done, Alleluia!
Fought the fight, the battle won, Alleluia!
Lo! the Sun's eclipse is over, Alleluia!
Lo! He sets in blood no more, Alleluia!

Hymns of praise then let us sing, Alleluia!
Unto Christ, our heavenly King, Alleluia!
Who endured the cross and grave, Alleluia!
Sinners to redeem and save. Alleluia!

Response: *Jesus, I sing your praises! Alleluia! You have risen! Your redeeming work is done. You have won the battle, burst the gates of hell, and opened paradise for me! There is no sting of death because you are victorious over the grave. Thank you for the glorious hope of the resurrection. Because you live, I, too, shall live eternally with you. Praise the Risen Lord!*

Works Cited

1. MacArthur, John, *The Murder of Jesus: A Study of How Jesus Died* (Nashville, TN: Thomas Nelson, 2000), 165.

2. Ibid., 176.

3. "Messiah in Passover," http://biblicalholidays.com.
Haidle, Helen, *Journey to the Cross: The Complete Easter Story for Young Readers* (Grand Rapids, MI: Zonderkidz, 2001), 117.

4. Zugibe, Frederick, *The Cross and the Shroud: A Medical Inquiry into the Crucifixion* (New York: Paragon House, 1988), 15–16.

5. Ibid., 15.

6. MacArthur, 183.

7. Strobel, Lee, *The Case for Christ: A Journalist's Personal Investigation of the Evidence for Jesus* (Grand Rapids, MI: Zondervan, 1998), 16.

8. Ibid., 14–15.

9. MacArthur, 192.

10. Zugibe, 24.

11. Ibid., 204.

12. Maier, Paul L., *In the Fullness of Time: A Historian Looks at Christmas, Easter, and the Early Church* (Grand Rapids, MI: Kregel, 1991), 167.

13. "Messiah in Passover," http://biblicalholidays.com.

14. MacArthur, 203–204.

15. Ibid., 196.

16. Ibid., 198.

17. Ray Vander Laan and Focus on the Family Video (That the World May Know Series), *Faith Lessons on the Death and Resurrection of the Messiah: City of the Great King (2)* (Grand Rapids, MI: Zondervan, 1997, 1998), Volume 4, Video 1.

18. Zugibe, 45–46.

19. MacArthur, 202.

20. *The MacArthur Study Bible* (Nashville, TN: Thomas Nelson, Word Publishing, 1997), 1449.

21. Zugibe, 206–207.

22. "Messiah in Passover," http://biblicalholidays.com.
Strobel, 18.

23. Strobel, 19.

24. "Messiah in Passover," http://biblicalholidays.com.
Zugibe, 207.
MacArthur, 200.

25. Strobel, 20–21.

26. MacArthur, 202–203.

27. MacArthur, 228.

28. Higgs, Liz Curtis, *Mad Mary: A Bad Girl from Magdala, Transformed at His Appearing* (Colorado Springs, CO: WaterBrook Press, 2001), 202.

29. Zugibe, 103.

30. *The MacArthur Study Bible,* 1625.

31. Bob Deffinbaugh, Th.M, "The Crucifixion (John 19:17–37)," http://www.bible.org.

32. Vander Laan and Focus on the Family Video (That the World May Know Series), *The True Easter Story: The Promise Kept* (Grand Rapids, MI: Zondervan, 2000).
Haidle, Helen, 154.

33. MacArthur, 231. (Miracles of Calvary Keathley)

34. Ibid., 231.

35. Ibid., 202, 239–240.

36. Zugibe, 84.

37. Lucado, Max, *The Final Week of Jesus* (Multnomah: Multnomah Books, 1994), 22.

38. Haidle, 165.

39. Vander Laan and Focus on the Family Video, *The True Easter Story: The Promise Kept.*

40. Haidle, 166.

41. Ibid., 171.

42. Ibid., 178.

43. Osbeck, Kenneth W., *Amazing Grace: 366 Inspiring Hymn Stories for Daily Devotions* (Grand Rapids, MI: Kregel, 1990), 127.

44. Maier, 180–181.

45. Ibid., 185.

46. Ibid., 205.

47. Yancey, Philip, *The Jesus I Never Knew* (Grand Rapids, MI: Zondervan, 1995), 219.

48. Omartian, Stormie, *The Power of a Praying Wife* (Eugene, Oregon: Harvest House, 1997), 19.

Where Do We Go from Here?

Monday: Meeting the Risen Savior
Mary Magdalene Part II

One day in heaven, I'd like to have a long talk with Mary Magdalene about those long hours after Jesus' died. What was she thinking? The death scene at the cross could have been the end for Mary Magdalene. Here is the AD 30 scene: Mary knows that Jesus is gone; to many it is time to move on. Instead, she returns to the tomb. And because of her commitment to the man who saved her from *hell on earth,* she witnesses the *glories of heaven.* In a beautiful and tender reunion, she is the first to see Jesus after His resurrection.

📖 Read John 20:11–18.

1. What does Mary's answer reveal about what she thinks has happened to her Lord (verse 13)?

_____

_____

2. What two questions does Jesus ask in verse 15?

_____

_____

When Mary responds that she doesn't know where her Lord is, she reveals that though she *sees* Jesus, she does not *recognize* Him. Mary assumes Jesus is a gardener, and perhaps this gardener has taken away the body. She does *not* experience immediate resurrection joy.

Then Jesus says, "Mary."

His voice must be unforgettable for when Mary hears her name, she cries out in Aramaic, *"Rabboni,"* addressing Him as "Teacher."

I cannot wait until I hear Jesus say *my* name. I cannot wait until I stand before Him and hear, *"Ann."* What about you? The most tender greeting you've experienced will pale in comparison to the love saturated in Jesus' voice when he sees you at the beginning of eternity. How will you react?

3. Jesus' next comment in John 20:17 indicates Mary's next reaction. How do you think Mary responded?

_____

A *woman* healed of seven demons is given the powerful news that Jesus has overcome Satan, the head of all demons, and has conquered death. A *woman* learns the news during a period of history when her testimony is considered invalid in most circles. And yet, Jesus tells Mary to go and tell![1]

Author Philip Yancey suggests if you're trying to build a case for the resurrection, you don't build it with unacceptable witnesses whose testimony will be questioned. But instead, the Gospel writers recorded the truth: women were the first witnesses of the resurrection.[2]

The Gospels agree on the primary facts. Mary Magdalene arrived at the tomb first, the tomb was open, the angels proclaimed the resurrection news, and Mary saw Jesus first.[3] Still, why did God give the most important news to inadmissible witnesses? I believe it's because of their commitment. Jesus honored those who followed Him every step of the way by revealing the greatest moment in history to them. Doesn't it make you want to take hold of Jesus' hand and not miss any part of the journey? What do we pass up if we're absent from the cross or the tomb?

Read Matthew 28:8–11 and Luke 24:9–11. These verses describe Jesus' appearance to the women.

4. What is the reaction of the women (Matthew 28:8–10)?

_____

_____

5. What is Jesus' instruction to the women (Matthew 28:10)?

_____

_____

> "When they heard that Jesus was alive and that she had seen him, *they did not believe it.*" (Mark 16:11)

6. What is the reaction of the eleven disciples (Luke 24:11)?

_____

_____

7. Matthew 28:11 reveals that the word has gotten out to more than just the followers of Jesus. Who else knows?

Read Matthew 28:11–15.

8. What deception do the chief priests and elders devise?

_____

_____

Today there are many deceptions and explanations for Jesus' alleged resurrection.

- The women actually saw a gardener instead of the risen Lord.
- The disciples moved the body.
- Jesus was never really dead; he was merely "swooning."
- The women and men were all seeing things.
- Joseph moved the body to another place.
- The women found the *wrong* empty tomb.
- The gardener moved the body.
- Romans stole the body.
- Jews stole the body.
- Jesus had a twin.

If Jesus never died, how does a badly damaged man get out of the grave with clothes plastered to His body, roll away a stone, walk miles on nail-pierced feet, and gain a following of cowering disciples?[4] And would those disciples actually risk their lives for a liar? Would the sheep who fled from their shepherd in the Garden of Gethsemane have the courage to stake *their* lives on the recreation of *His*? They're not even good enough actors to pretend He's resurrected!

Yes, the tomb has been unguarded from the time Joseph rolled the stone in front of the tomb until the time the soldiers secured it. But who would steal a dead body?[5] Nobody doubts that the body is *missing*; the question should be, "Where is the body?" The religious leaders only need to flaunt Jesus' body to end all the discussion and the growth of Christianity. And so their excuse that the disciples have *stolen* it further confirms that the tomb is *empty*.[6]

The truth is this: The tomb is empty because Jesus rose from the dead in the same body that was buried.[7] Whether we choose to accept it or not does not take away the simple truth that Jesus was born, lived, died, and rose again for all who believe, and the head that once was crowned with thorns is now crowned with glory!

"The Head That Once Was Crowned with Thorns," verses 1, 6:

The head that once was crowned with thorns is crowned with glory now;
A royal diadem adorns the mighty Victor's brow.

The cross he bore is life and health, though shame and death to him,
His people's hope, His people's wealth, their everlasting theme.

Jesus' Words in Action: Did Jesus rise from the dead? If we answer "no," then we need to find answers to the following questions and more:

- Why was the body unwrapped before it was stolen?
- Why would guards leave their station?
- Why weren't the disciples punished for *stealing* the body?
- Why weren't the guards executed for allowing the body to be stolen?

There are simply too many questions that need to be answered if Jesus did not rise from the dead. He is the Resurrection and the Life. He said it (John 11:25). Believe it!

Tuesday: Sunday Afternoon with the Savior

📖 Read Luke 24:13–29.

It's Sunday afternoon, and two men are walking the seven-mile journey *away* from Jerusalem to Emmaus (see map on p. 16). As they review the sad events of their weekend, they are downcast and miserable, obviously *not* awaiting any proof of the resurrection. This scene is easily transferred to script format. We can hear the dialogue as Jesus converses with the two men.

I once wrote a church sermon skit about the journey to Emmaus. In the dialogue, when Jesus acts unaware about the headlines in Jerusalem, the two men are incredulous about His ignorance and question, "Where've you been? Under a rock or something?"

But in *Luke's* script they ask, "Are you only a visitor to Jerusalem and do not know the things that have happened there in these days?" (Luke 24:18). Indeed, Jesus is a *visitor* to earth. *Heaven* is His home, but He's hanging around to teach a few more lessons to make His resurrection real to many!

1. According to Luke 24:19, what do these two men know about Jesus?

_____

_____

2. What did they hope Jesus would do (verse 21)?

_____

_____

3. In Week Five, we studied what the disciples were told by Jesus about His death and resurrection. The men on the walk to Emmaus tell their companion what they should recognize as the fulfillment of Jesus' prophecy. List the points below (verses 21–24).

_____

_____

4. Jesus must have been exasperated. The two are walking away from hope! But when do *we* know Jesus' promises and still walk away from them? Can you share a time when you've turned away from His extended arms?

_____

_____

Jesus chastises their foolishness and their lack of belief in what the prophets have spoken (verses 25–26). He then explains *all* of the Scriptures concerning Himself beginning with Moses and all the Prophets. Remember the Old Testament passages we looked at last week that prophesied events surrounding Christ's death? Wouldn't it be great to hear it from Jesus Himself? You *can*! The Word of God is still here for us to study so we never walk away from hope!

Still they do not recognize Him. But when Jesus *acts* like He's going beyond the village, the men strongly urge Him to stay on with them (verse 29).

📖 Read Luke 24:30–44.

> "And beginning with Moses and all the Prophets, he explained to them what was said in all the Scriptures concerning himself." (Luke 24:27)

5. What causes the men to see Jesus (verses 30–31)?

_____

When Jesus breaks bread and gives thanks, something clicks. Their eyes are opened, they recognize Him, and poof— He disappears. They comment after their Sabbath of Sunday School stories and sermons, "Were not our hearts burning within us while he talked with us on the road and opened the Scriptures to us?" (Luke 24:32).

Indeed! When Jesus talks and the Scriptures are opened, we, too, should feel that kind of excitement! Would you like to have the Scriptures opened to *you*? You have more Scripture available to you than these two men did. All you have to do is open your Bible! Walk and talk with Jesus just like these two did on their journey!

Now they have a clue and know what to do. They get up and return *at once* to Jerusalem.

6. Complete what they tell the eleven disciples and others gathered with them. "It is _____! The _____ has _____ and has _____ to Simon" (verse 34).

Can you imagine the joy of retelling the story of the journey, Jesus' prophecies, and revelations? And then as if to put an exclamation point at the end of the story, Jesus Himself appears and says, "Peace be with you" (verse 36).

As I write studies, I'm often filled with angst over deadlines and accuracy. It would be wonderful to hear His gentle voice say, "Peace be with you, Ann."

7. But how does Luke describe their emotions? Do they experience resurrection joy (verse 37)?

_____

8. What does Jesus ask of them (Luke 24:39)?

_____

9. *Now* what is their reaction to Him (Luke 24:41)?

_____

10. In the midst of joy, amazement, and awe, I think it's humorous that Jesus asks if there is anything to eat. What a guy thing (Luke 24:41)! But why might Jesus have chosen that moment to dine?

_____

While His very real body feasts on broiled fish, Jesus explains that He fulfills Old Testament prophecy.

Do you see how it's all fitting together? What a perfect close to our lesson about knowing Scriptures and walking closely with Jesus.

The two men on the journey to Emmaus know Jesus' prophecy but walk *away* from hope. Sometimes when we are most distraught, we feel Jesus is no longer there. Each time I think of the journey of these two men, I remember my dear friends Denny and Laura, who took another kind of journey to Emmaus.

> "This is what I told you while I was still with you: Everything must be fulfilled that is written about me in the Law of Moses, the Prophets and the Psalms." (Luke 24:44)

After repeated *in vitro* attempts and one miscarriage, Denny and Laura were told they were expecting a baby. They had high hopes and dreams for their child. Being strong musicians, they could imagine their child as an accomplished musician. They looked forward to providing a warm and nurturing home, only to discover that they were actually pregnant with twins, but one had died *in utero*. They later found out that the surviving baby was a girl with Down's Syndrome.

They were devastated. On the day Laura received the diagnosis, their daughter kicked for the first time. Laura is an inquisitive person, so she looked around the hospital cafeteria for anyone who might be in a similar situation. *Where do they hide all the Down's Syndrome kids?* she asked herself. She needed to talk.

Denny was cautious, distant, and angry. He wasn't sure this baby was meant to be. He had recently lost his father and his brother and now looked forward to a new family. He didn't want any more pain. Besides, this child might have a terrible life. And maybe this child would alter their marriage in ways he couldn't imagine. He was so weary with grief.

As the couple's days of crying turned to weeks of sadness and indecision, Laura attended a retreat on joy and began to hope she'd again feel joy. Though the two questioned, "Where is Jesus right now?" they slowly began to feel His gentle presence. They began to understand and relate to the two men on the journey to Emmaus who thought Jesus was far away when He was walking right there beside them.

Their daughter was born on January 18, 2000, a tiny, beautiful blonde-haired angel. Indeed, she altered their marriage and their lives in ways they couldn't imagine. Though their daughter has Down's Syndrome, she is healthy. Denny and Laura knew Jesus had journeyed with them through the nine months, so they gave their daughter a name that would forever remind them of His presence and joy. They named her *Emma and Us—Emmaus Joy.*

Laura likes to show off a picture of Emma at the age of two standing in front of a mirror in her flower girl dress (one of *three* weddings in which Emma was the flower girl!). Emma is admiring herself in her pretty dress. Standing behind her, also in the reflection, is the face of her father. That's the part Laura loves best. Denny was transformed. Oh, the love on Emma's Daddy's face! Emma Joy may not always fully grasp the depth of it, but her father's love and joy is mirrored there.

I could tell you plenty about the joyous miracles Emmaus Joy has brought Denny and Laura. But you don't need any more except those created by God for you when you put your hand in His. Nobody but Jesus can give you the peace and joy on your journey that Laura and Denny experienced.

Jesus' Words in Action: Can you say that *your* heart burns with a desire to know Him more? Do you have that sweet communion? Do you feel the peace of having Him beside you? Try spending quality time with Him! Do you know that your heavenly Father is looking at you with love and joy? Even when you don't see Him in a tangible picture, He's there. How great is His love for you!

Maybe you wonder if Jesus is on the journey with you. Perhaps you're even walking away from your Jerusalem and the hope of resurrection. Turn back toward hope and the One who will journey with you in joy. Turn back to the One whose love is mirrored in every look at you. And if you're afraid you just can't find the way, pray to God that the scales on your eyes will fall off. Ask Him to show you signs of spring and hope!

Wednesday: Side-by-Side with the Savior

Today let's look at a few more encounters with Jesus. When Jesus first appears to the disciples, Thomas is not with them. After the disciples give Thomas an update, he lives up to his "Doubting Thomas" moniker. Lest we be too hard on Thomas, let's remember that back when the other disciples reminded Jesus of the danger of returning to Jerusalem (John 11:8), Thomas said, "Let us also go, that we may die with him" (John 11:11).

📖 Read John 20:24–29.

A week later the disciples convene and Thomas is with them. Let's eavesdrop on their locked door session.

1. What does Jesus say to the disciples when He unexpectedly appears without opening a door (verse 26)?

_____

_____

2. Thomas doesn't say anything, but Jesus knows what Thomas needs in order to believe. What does Jesus say Thomas should do (verse 27)?

_____

_____

> "Unless I see the nail marks in his hands and put my finger where the nails were, and put my hand into his side, I will not believe it."
> (John 20:25)

3. Do we know whether Thomas put his finger in Jesus' nail-pierced hands or reached out and put his hand in Jesus' side? What would it feel like to be Thomas and see the risen Lord and hear your own remark thrown back at you?

_____

_____

4. There is only one response Thomas can make. Record it below (John 20:28).

_____

5. Why are Jesus' words in John 20:27 and 29 for us as well?

_____

6. Do we believe without seeing? Do you find yourself doubting and need to hear Jesus' words, "Stop doubting and believe"? Consider the man in Mark 9:24 who begs Jesus, "I do believe; help me overcome my unbelief!" Faith as small as a mustard seed is powerful. Ask God to help grow your faith

(Matthew 17:20; Luke 17:6). Remember, doubt is not the opposite of faith; disobedience is.

_____

_____

Some time later, Jesus appears for a third time when the disciples are fishing. What joy the disciples must feel to have Jesus spend His day with them. I love the way John opens his story, "It happened this way. . . ."

📖 Read John 21:1–14.

7. Which disciples are present at this unsuccessful fishing expedition (verse 2)?

_____

_____

When Jesus appears on the shore and calls out, "Friends, haven't you any fish?" they do not recognize Him. He instructs them to throw their net on the right side of the boat in order to find some (verses 4–6). I'm not a fisherman, but I wonder, *why would the fish choose one side over the other?*

The fruit (or fish) of their obedience is beyond anything they could imagine. At this point John recognizes Jesus and declares, "It is the Lord!" (John 21:7). Peter impulsively puts his coat back on and jumps into the water, leaving the disciples to tow the net full of fish for the remaining hundred yards.

8. Why would Peter impulsively jump out of the boat to greet the Lord?

_____

_____

9. What are some of the miraculous aspects of this catch (John 20:11)?

_____

_____

Jesus has prepared a fire of burning coals and a meal of fish and bread. Are the disciples remembering when their Lord took a few loaves and fish and fed five thousand? This time He serves them a personal breakfast on the beach. This scene closes with an even more intimate scene between drenched Peter and the Master he previously denied three times.

📖 Read John 21:15–17.

10. What are Jesus' three questions to Peter?

1.

2.

3.

What are Peter's three answers?

1.

2.

3.

11. What two things does Jesus ask Peter to do with his love for Him (John 21:15–17)?

_____

John has followed Peter and joined the two. This scene closes with prophecies alluding to Peter and John's deaths. As stated earlier, John was probably the last disciple to die; traditional sources report Peter was martyred in AD 67 in Rome.[8]

Jesus' Words in Action: Have you ever made critical mistakes like Thomas and Peter? Although Thomas doubted, Jesus knew exactly what would bring him to faith. Although Peter denied Jesus—even after being forewarned, Jesus knew Peter would become a rock on which to build the church (Matthew 16:18). On Friday we'll look at Paul, a man who persecuted Christians in the early church. Jesus still used these three, because Jesus gives second, third, and fourth chances.

If you've doubted or denied Jesus and you want a fresh start, begin anew today. Jump into the water to rejoin the Lord and spend a breakfast with Him in prayer. Open the Word and ask for forgiveness and a fresh start. Jesus invites you to join Him for fellowship and a good walk on the beach. He has a plan for your life. Talk to Him about it today.

Thursday: Ascension and the Gift of the Holy Spirit

Jesus has been with His followers for *forty* days. Forty is a number laden with historical significance. This number is attached to numerous biblical events, such as the duration of the flood (40 days and 40 nights), Jesus' fast in the wilderness (40 days), Elijah's stay on the mountain (40 days), and the number of years wandering in the desert. During this forty-day period following His resurrection, Jesus appeared at least twelve times and to at least five hundred people.[9] We've read that Jesus was seen, heard, touched, and, on at least four occasions, He ate with His friends.[10]

Today we'll look at Jesus' final appearances on earth: the commission, the ascension, followed by Pentecost. Place bookmarks at Matthew 28:16, Luke 24:45, and Acts 1. Today we will read a number of short passages.

📖 Read Matthew 28:16–20.

1. Jesus meets the eleven disciples at a mountain in Galilee. Verse 17 says that some worship and some doubt. What do you suppose they doubt?

_____

_____

2. According to Matthew 28:18–20, with all the authority on heaven and earth, what does Jesus command?

_____

3. What promise accompanies the commission (verse 20)?

_____

📖 Read Luke 24:45–53.

4. *Where* are they to begin preaching (verse 47)?

_____

Who will assist them (verse 49)?

_____

When are they to act on their instructions (verse 49)?

I wonder what it would mean to be *clothed with power from on high* (verse 49). Do you think they understand *this* prophecy *this* time? Let's read on and find out!

📖 Read Acts 1:6–11.

5. What still concerns the disciples (Acts 1:6)?

_____

_____

They are not to worry about the *time*; instead, Jesus gives them important instructions. They will receive power when the Holy Spirit comes upon them (verse 8). Their witness will encompass Jerusalem, extend to Judea and Samaria, and then to the "ends of the earth." If you draw a circle around Jerusalem, then a wider concentric circle including the provinces, and finally the whole world, you can see the visual picture Jesus was drawing.

Jesus would instruct me, "Go tell others about Jesus in Paeonian Springs, in Loudoun and Fairfax Counties, Virginia, West Virginia, the United States, and in the whole world." What are your instructions? Where could you witness about Christ's death and resurrection?

When Jesus disappears yet again, they continue to stare up at the sky. Do they realize this time His departure is permanent? Or are they thinking He'll show up again on the beach, in a locked room, or on a mountain?

6. Who appears, and in your own words, what do they say (Acts 1:11)?

_____

_____

Jesus is coming back the same way He left. We have something big to prepare *for* and look forward *to*. His second coming will be a glorious event! Like the ten virgins, we need to have oil in our lamps and be ready for His return.

> "After the Lord Jesus had spoken to them, he was taken up into heaven and he sat at the right hand of God." (Mark 16:19)
>

The disciples couldn't just stand on the mountain and wait. So after worshiping Him, they "returned to Jerusalem with great joy." They "stayed continually at the temple, praising God," and the disciples and the women along with Mary, and Jesus' brothers "joined together constantly in prayer" (Luke 24:52–53; Acts 1:12–14).

If they fully understood the Old Testament prophecy, they could rejoice that Jesus, the high priest, is seated at the right hand of God making intercession for us.

📖 Read Acts 1:1–5, which introduces us to the gift of the Holy Spirit.

Luke authored both Luke and Acts. In the opening of Acts, Luke records a specific and crucial command that Jesus made while on earth.

7. Fill in the blanks below. "Do not leave _____,

but wait for the _____ my Father promised, which you have heard me speak about. For John _____ with _____, but in a few days you will be baptized with the _____ _____" (Acts 1:4–5).

Would the disciples wonder what it meant to be baptized with the *Holy Spirit*? The end of Luke also gives instructions about *waiting* for the Holy Spirit.

Pentecost falls fifty days (*Pente = fifty*) after Passover and celebrates the harvest's first fruits. Jerusalem would have been crowded with visitors from around the world for this event. The gift of the Holy Spirit occurs at Pentecost. Let's see how Pentecost and the gift of the Holy Spirit intersect.

Read Acts 2:1–13.

Verse one indicates *"they were all together in one place."* This would include both men and women experiencing an amazing event.

> "Therefore he is able to save completely those who come to God through him, because he always lives to intercede for them." (Hebrews 7:25)

> "I am going to send you what my Father has promised; but stay in the city until you have been clothed with power from on high." (Luke 24:49)

_____

_____

8. How is the event described (verses 2–3)?

_____

_____

9. What are they able to do after they are filled with the Holy Spirit (verse 4)?

_____

_____

10. "Many God-fearing Jews from every nation under heaven" (verse 5) are in Jerusalem at the time. How many regions are represented (verses 5, 9, 10–11)?

_____

The visitors to Jerusalem are amazed and perplexed. The Galileans are speaking native languages from a list of places and "declaring the wonders of God" (Acts 2:11). Some critics are appalled and think they are just drunk.

11. Would you be surprised if I told you this event was also prophesied? Read on in Joel 2 and underline what you see in

the Old Testament about the gift of the Holy Spirit.

And afterward, I will pour out my Spirit on all people. Your sons and daughters will prophesy, your old men will dream dreams, your young men will see visions. Even on my servants, both men and women, I will pour out my Spirit in those days. I will show wonders in the heavens and on the earth, blood and fire and billows of smoke (Joel 2:28–30).

This is another incident where Jesus fulfills prophecy and replaces old festivals with new celebrations. It is no accident that all Old Testament holidays are, or will be, replaced by Jesus. Jesus IS the celebration!

How Jesus Fulfills the Celebrations[11]

Jesus' Words in Action: Before Christ's death, He instructs His followers to be ready for His return by telling the Parable

Spring Festivals:	**First Coming**
Passover (Leviticus 23:4–8)	Lord's Supper (1 Corinthians 5:7–8)
Feast of Unleavened Bread	Crucifixion, Seed planted at beginning of Feast
Feast of First Fruits (Leviticus 23:11)	Resurrection – first fruits! (1 Corinthians 15:20, 23)
Feast of Weeks – 7 weeks harvest	Pentecost/Holy Spirit – 50 days
Fall Festivals:	**Second Coming**
Feast of Trumpets (Leviticus 23:23–24)	Jesus' Second Coming (1 Thessalonians 4:16–17)
Day of Atonement (Leviticus 23:26–28)	Judgment (Romans 3:23–25)
Feast of Tabernacles	Second Coming (Micah 4:1); Jesus lives among us

of the Ten Bridesmaids (see Matthew 25:1–13). We studied His comments about marriage at the Last Passover and in the garden. Though the women have lanterns, some are not prepared with enough oil for the bridegroom's return. He consistently describes His relationship to us as a marriage. Are you committed? Do you have oil in your lamp? Are you awake and ready for Christ's return? Will you be ready to celebrate the Feast?

> "The Spirit and the bride say, 'Come!' And let him who hears say, 'Come!' Whoever is thirsty, let him come; and whoever wishes, let him take the free gift of the water of life." (Revelation 22:17)
>
>

Friday: The Holy Spirit in the Lives of Believers

I love a good "before and after" story complete with photographs. We've studied how Jesus changed the lives of many women and men. Today we'll see how the gift of the Holy Spirit does extreme makeovers on Christians in the early church.

1. Under *Verses from Acts 2* in the outline below, list the verses for each topic.

Topic: Verses from Acts 2:14–36

I.   No, we're not drunk at 9:00 a.m. in the morning. (14–15)
II. Joel prophesied this.
III. This is what *you* did to Jesus of Nazareth.
IV. King David prophesied about his descendant.
V.   The prophecy has been fulfilled (29–36).

Let's focus on Topic III from the outline above and answer a few questions about Peter's retelling of what happened to Jesus. According to Peter's statement in verses 22–24, God is responsible for miracles, signs, and wonders; knew before time all that would happen; and raised Jesus from the dead. But Peter doesn't mince words. Over and over he points out who is responsible for Jesus' death.

> "You killed the author of life, but God raised him from the dead. We are witnesses of this." (Acts 3:15)

Peter has no doubts or fear, but what about his audience? They were "cut to the heart" and asked, "Brothers, what shall we do?" (Acts 2:37).

Read Acts 2:37–41.

2. Peter has the solution. What is his answer?

"_____ and be _____, every one of you, in the name of _____ _____ for the _____ of your _____. And you will receive the gift of the _____ _____. The promise is for you and your children and for all who are far off—for all whom the _____ our _____ will call." (Acts 2:38–39)

This sounds like Jesus' prophecy fulfilled. Jesus prophesied to the disciples before His ascension, telling them to stay in Jerusalem until they had been clothed with power from on high. After that they would preach repentance and forgiveness, beginning in Jerusalem (Luke 24:46–49).

Now they're clothed with power from on high, and it's making a big difference! And following that Feast of Weeks, we see the *first fruits of the harvest.* Three thousand are added to the faith that day.

Though the Sanhedrin doesn't like the growth of the church and imprisons and persecutes Christians, its members are timid about creating martyrs.[12] Peter is arrested, and the number of believers grows to five thousand (Acts 4:4). After being freed, Peter continues to expound with prophecy, finger pointing (Acts 4:10–11), and then concludes with the ultimate answer, "Salvation is found in no one else, for there is no other name under heaven given to men by which we must be saved" (Acts 4:12).

Could we be so bold? What is the ultimate reaction?

When they saw the courage of Peter and John and realized that they were unschooled, ordinary men, they were astonished and they took note that these men had been with Jesus. (Acts 4:13)

The Sanhedrin then asks, "What are we going to do with these men?" (Acts 4:16). Though they warn these men *not* to teach in the name of Jesus, Peter and John answer (my paraphrase) "No way! We're gonna preach Jesus! We can't *help* talking about what He has done!" (Acts 4:19–20).

Similarly, after *another* imprisonment followed by a miraculous release (Acts 5:17–28), Peter and the other apostles explain why they continue to preach repentance, forgiveness, and obedience (Acts 5:29–32), saying, "We must obey God rather than men!"

This growing church, dependent on the Holy Spirit, rocks the world. According to Frank Morrison,

> Within twenty years the claim of these Galilean peasants had disrupted the Jewish church and impressed itself upon every town on the Eastern littoral of the Mediterranean from Caesarea to Troas. In

> **Jesus' Prophecy Fulfilled:** "I tell you the truth, unless a kernel of wheat falls to the ground and dies, it remains only a single seed. But if it dies, it produces many seeds." (John 12:24)
>
>

less than fifty years it had begun to threaten the peace of the Roman Empire.[13]

How would a group with that kind of faith look as a community of believers? Let's find out in the next two passages.

📖 Read Acts 2:42–47; 4:32–37.

3. List the many *bodybuilding* activities that bring Christians together in the early church.

_____

_____

4. What would it be like to be a woman in this growing, sharing, grace-filled church with members who are one in heart and mind?

_____

_____

5. Which of the women we studied in Weeks Two and Three do you want to read about in service and worship in the early church?

_____

_____

> "All the believers were one in heart and mind. No one claimed that any of his possessions was his own, but they shared everything they had." (Acts 4:32)

Women are listed throughout the New Testament as they worship and serve in the early church. Perhaps in future study, you may want to read these accounts (Acts 1:14; 2:18; 5:14; 16:13–15, 40; 17:12; Romans 16:1–4, 6, 12, 13, 15).

Now note the emphasis on *both men and women.*

The early church grows with *both men and women* believers (Acts 5:14).

Both men and women are baptized (Acts 8:12).

Both men and women receive the Holy Spirit and prophesy in accordance with prophecy (Acts 2:18).

Both men and women of different backgrounds are taught. Prominent women, many of whom are Gentiles, are added to the church (Acts 17:4, 12), and now the apostles actually teach *women* (Acts 16:13). (Do you see a difference from your first week's study of women and religion?)

Both men and women of this early church are persecuted. *Both men and women* believers are dragged off and put in prison (Acts 8:3).

Both male and female followers of the Way are persecuted by Paul (Acts 22:4).

Let's take a look at Paul, who is another witness to the resurrection of Jesus.

In Acts 9, Paul meets Jesus on the road to Damascus. Paul was literally on a journey (verse 3), yet not a journey to seek out the risen Savior. Paul was formerly a persecutor of that fledgling group of believers called "The Way." But Jesus chose Paul, and Paul believed the revelation and answered, "Who are you, Lord?" (verse 5). He then obeyed God's direction (verse 6).

Paul proclaims Christ's resurrection in 1 Corinthians 15:3–8:

> *For what I received I passed on to you as of first importance: that Christ died for our sins according to the Scriptures, that he was buried, that he was raised on the third day according to the Scriptures, and that he appeared to Peter, and then to the Twelve. After that, he appeared to more than five hundred of the brothers at the same time, most of whom are still living, though some have fallen asleep. Then he appeared to James, then to all the apostles, and last of all he appeared to me also, as to one abnormally born.*

It is Paul who makes these points:

"And if Christ has not been raised, our preaching is useless and so is your faith." (1 Corinthians 15:14)

"And if Christ has not been raised, your faith is futile; you are still in your sins." (1 Corinthians 15:17)

"If only for this life we have hope in Christ, we are to be pitied more than all men." (1 Corinthians 15:19)

God used Paul's faith and witness to spread the Gospel. Just listen to Paul declare who Jesus is. Underline all titles and descriptions of Jesus.

> *He is the image of the invisible God, the firstborn over all creation. For by him all things were created: things in heaven and on earth, visible and invisible, whether thrones or powers or rulers or authorities; all*

things were created by him and for him. He is before all things, and in him all things hold together. And he is the head of the body, the church; he is the beginning and the firstborn from among the dead, so that in everything he might have the supremacy. For God was pleased to have all his fullness dwell in him, and through him to reconcile to himself all things, whether things on earth or things in heaven, by making peace through his blood, shed on the cross. (Colossians 1:15–20)

Paul would come to glory only in the cross, and he often wrote about its power. Let's close our study by looking at New Testament writings about the cross, the blood, and discipleship.

The Cross

"For the message of the cross is foolishness to those who are perishing, but to us who are being saved it is the power of God." (1 Corinthians 1:18)

"May I never boast except in the cross of our Lord Jesus Christ, through which the world has been crucified to me, and I to the world." (Galatians 6:14)

"He himself bore our sins in his body on the tree, so that we might die to sins and live for righteousness; by his wounds you have been healed." (1 Peter 2:24)

6. What does the cross mean to *you*? After these eight weeks, what new thoughts have you gained about it?

_____

_____

_____

_____

The Blood

"In him we have redemption through his blood, the forgiveness of sins, in accordance with the riches of God's grace that he lavished on us with all wisdom and understanding." (Ephesians 1:7–8)

"How much more, then, will the blood of Christ, who through the eternal Spirit offered himself unblemished to God, cleanse our consciences from acts that lead to death, so that we may serve the living God!" (Hebrews 9:14)

"But if we walk in the light, as he is in the light, we have fellowship with one another, and the blood of Jesus, his Son, purifies us from all sin." (1 John 1:7)

7. What does the blood mean to you? What new thoughts have you gained about it?

Discipleship

Then Jesus said to his disciples, "If anyone would come after me, he must deny himself and take up his cross and follow me. For whoever wants to save his life will lose it, but whoever loses his life for me will find it. What good will it be for a man if he gains the whole world, yet forfeits his soul? Or what can a man give in exchange for his soul?" (Matthew 16:24–26)

Now if we are children, then we are heirs—heirs of God and co-heirs with Christ, if indeed we share in his sufferings in order that we may also share in his glory. I consider that our present sufferings are not worth comparing with the glory that will be revealed in us. (Romans 8:17–18)

8. What does it mean to be a follower of Christ? What does it mean to share in His sufferings?

_____

_____

9. Why is it necessary to journey to the cross and also to journey beyond?

_____

Peter was sifted, tested, persecuted, imprisoned, and then spoke out about the goal of faith: the salvation of souls. We see that the faith of female followers was also tested through imprisonment and persecution. We, too, can know our faith will be tested and that we will face persecution for being followers of Christ.

📖 Read 1 Peter 1:3–9.

10. What happens when your faith is tested (1 Peter 1:7)?

> "But rejoice that you participate in the sufferings of Christ, so that you may be overjoyed when his glory is revealed." (1 Peter 4:13)
>
>

Minister George Bennard answered his trials with a song. When he went through a difficult period, he considered the meaning of the cross and what it meant to share in Christ's suffering. After much study, reflection, and prayer, he wrote,

> I saw the Christ of the cross as if I were seeing John 3:16 leave the printed page, take form and act out the meaning of redemption. The more I contemplated these truths the more convinced I became that the cross was far more than just a religious symbol but rather the very heart of the gospel.[14]

These reflections inspired the hymn "The Old Rugged Cross."

"The Old Rugged Cross"

On a hill far away stood an old rugged cross, the emblem of suf-
f'ring and shame;
And I love that old cross where the dearest and best for a world of
lost sinners was slain.

O that old rugged cross, so despised by the world, has a wondrous
attraction for me;
For the dear Lamb of God left His glory above to bear it to dark
Calvary.

To the old rugged cross I will ever be true, its shame and reproach
gladly bear;
Then He'll call me some day to my home far away, where His glory
forever I'll share.

So I'll cherish the old rugged cross, till my trophies at last I lay
down;
I will cling to the old rugged cross, and exchange it some day for a
crown.

Jesus' Words in Action: Where are you on your journey now? Do you understand the blood, the cross, the sacrifice, and the ultimate glory? In the introduction to this study, you read the chorus of the hymn "Lead Me to Calvary" by Jennie Hussey and William Kirkpatrick. The verses are so appropriate here:

King of my life I crown Thee now—Thine shall the glory be;
Lest I forget Thy thorn-crowned brow, lead me to Calvary.

May I be willing, Lord, to bear daily my cross for Thee;
Even Thy cup of grief to share—Thou hast borne all for me.

Lest I forget Gethsemane, lest I forget Thine agony,
Lest I forget Thy love for me, lead me to Calvary.

Are you ready to participate in His sufferings and in His glory? Do you understand that the Holy Spirit has been left with you, too? Can you move beyond Resurrection Sunday with renewed vision of who your Savior is, and that Jesus loved you and still loves you, and will love you no matter what you do? You are a woman created by God, loved by God and encouraged by God to grow in relationship with Him.

> *Your attitude should be the same as that of Christ Jesus: Who, being in very nature God, did not consider equality with God something to be grasped, but made himself nothing, taking the very nature of a servant, being made in human likeness. And being found in appearance as a man, he humbled himself and became obedient to death—even death on a cross! Therefore God exalted him to the highest place and gave him the name that is above every name, that at the name of Jesus every knee should bow, in heaven and on earth and under the earth, and every tongue confess that Jesus Christ is Lord, to the glory of God the Father. (Philippians 2:5–11)*

Saturday: "Are You Washed in the Blood of the Lamb?" by Elisha Hoffman

Scriptures: "At that time the kingdom of heaven will be like ten virgins who took their lamps and went out to meet the bridegroom. Five of them were foolish and five were wise. The foolish ones took their lamps but did not take any oil with them. The wise, however, took oil in jars along with their lamps." (Matthew 25:1–4)

"Are You Washed in the Blood of the Lamb?" is one of my favorite Easter hymns. It celebrates the paradox of being as white as snow by being washed in the blood of the Lamb. Verse 3 focuses on the ten virgins and being ready for Jesus' second coming. Are you ready? Have you been washed in the blood of the Lamb? When your bridegroom returns will you be clothed in white? Spend a minute answering each question in this song.

"Are You Washed in the Blood of the Lamb?"

Have you been to Jesus for the cleansing power?
Are you washed in the blood of the Lamb?
Are you fully trusting in His grace this hour?
Are you washed in the blood of the Lamb?

Are you walking daily by the Savior's side?
Are you washed in the blood of the Lamb?
Do you rest each moment in the Crucified?
Are you washed in the blood of the Lamb?

When the Bridegroom cometh will your robes be white?
Are you washed in the blood of the Lamb?
Will your soul be ready for the mansions bright,
And be washed in the blood of the Lamb?

Lay aside the garments that are stained with sin,
And be washed in the blood of the Lamb;
There's a fountain flowing for the soul unclean,
O be washed in the blood of the Lamb!

CHORUS:

Are you washed in the blood,
In the soul cleansing blood of the Lamb?
Are your garments spotless? Are they white as snow?
Are you washed in the blood of the Lamb?

> Are you walking daily by the Savior's side?
> Are you washed in the blood of the Lamb?
>
> "Are You Washed in the Blood of the Lamb?" Elisha Hoffman

Response: *Lord Jesus, make my garments as white as snow. As I walk beside you, let me trust in you every hour of the day. May my greatest longing be to see You face to face. Thank you for washing me in the blood of the Lamb!*

Sunday: "Rejoice the Lord Is King!"

Scripture: "Rejoice in the Lord always. I will say it again: Rejoice!" (Philippians 4:4)

We have arrived. "Rejoice the Lord is King!" He has purged our stains and taken a seat at the right hand of God! This hymn by Charles Wesley, like so many hymns, celebrates

Jesus' second coming when we shall hear the trump of God sound. Rejoice!

"Rejoice the Lord Is King!"

Rejoice the Lord is King! Your Lord and King adore!
Rejoice, give thanks and sing, and triumph ever-
more.
Jesus, the Savior reigns, the God of truth and love:
When he had purged our stains, he took his seat
above.

His kingdom cannot fail; he rules o'er earth and heaven;
The keys of death and hell are to our Jesus given.

He sits at God's right hand till all his foes submit,
And bow to his command, and fall beneath his feet:

Rejoice in glorious hope! Jesus the Judge shall come
And take his servants up to their eternal home:
We soon shall hear the archangel's voice, the trump of God shall
sound: rejoice!

Let this final hymn endure well beyond our last day together.

"Crown Him with Many Crowns!"
By Matthew Bridges and Godfrey Thring

Crown Him with many crowns, the Lamb upon His throne:
Hark! How the heav'nly anthem drowns all music but its own!
Awake, my soul, and sing of Him who died for thee,
And hail Him as thy matchless King thru all eternity.

Crown Him the Lord of love: Behold His hands and side—
Rich wounds, yet visible above, in beauty glorified;
No angel in the sky can fully bear that sight,
But downward bends his wond'ring eye at mysteries so bright.

Crown Him the Lord of life:
Who triumphed o'er the grave,
Who rose victorious to the strife for those He came to save;
His glories now we sing, who died and rose on high,
Who died eternal life to bring and lives that death may die.

Closing Thoughts

My heart is not quite prepared to say good-bye. We are at the end of this journey, but thankfully our journey continues into

> *Lift up your heart!*
> *Lift up your voice!*
> *Rejoice! Again I say, rejoice!*
>
> "Rejoice the Lord is King" by Charles Wesley

eternity, where together we'll walk with Jesus.

If you now looked back at the list of women on page 25, who would you relate to? Are you reaching for Jesus' tassel? Are you ready to anoint His head and feet? Can you sit at Jesus' feet and learn from Him?

What is your plan of study after these eight weeks? Perhaps you'll choose to focus on the entire ministry of Christ through one Gospel or continue on with the early church in Acts and Romans. Maybe prophecy intrigues you. If so, try Isaiah. Or perhaps the New Testament book of Hebrews offers a challenging perspective on merging the Old and the New Testaments. AMG Publishers has published two studies on women of the Bible (see Following God™ Bible studies at www.amgpublishers.com).

Do you need someone to help and encourage you in your spiritual walk? Join a study with other women. Do you need someone to mentor you? Ask. Or perhaps a new believer needs you as a mentor.

I was in a meeting where the directors were discussing new children's programs. At last one desperate mom replied, "*I* need that class. *I* don't know all of that stuff and *I* need to know more." Because of her vulnerability, two more women confessed their hunger for the Word. Someone encouraged them, "Watch for someone around you that loves the Word. Ask that person to study with you and mentor you. Get in an accountability group so you can pray for each other and grow together! Exciting things are about to happen!"

It wasn't long before an effervescent young woman in the church was leading these women and running alongside to keep up with their enthusiasm. Maybe you need to be part of a group like theirs. Take someone's hand and learn as you lead, or be mentored. You'll be thrilled with what happens to your faith.

I loved taking this journey with you. I may never meet you on earth, but one day our journey on earth will conclude with a glorious reunion in heaven! We will stand before the Lord because, as the song by Elvina Hall says, "Jesus Paid it All."

"Jesus Paid It All"

Jesus paid it all, All to Him I owe;
Sin has left a crimson stain, He washed it white as snow.

And when before the throne—I stand in Him complete,
I'll lay my trophies down—All down at Jesus' feet.

My closing prayer for you comes directly from Hebrews 13:20–21.

> *May the God of peace, who through the blood of the eternal covenant brought back from the dead our Lord Jesus, that great Shepherd of the sheep, equip you with everything good for doing his will, and may he work in us what is pleasing to him, through Jesus Christ, to whom be glory for ever and ever. Amen.*

Works Cited

1. Richards, Sue and Larry, *Every Woman in the Bible* (Nashville, TN: Thomas Nelson, 1999), 162.

2. Yancey, Philip, *The Jesus I Never Knew* (Grand Rapids, MI: Zondervan, 1995), 212.

Maier, Paul L., *In the Fullness of Time: A Historian Looks at Christmas, Easter, and the Early Church* (Grand Rapids, MI: Kregel, 1991,) 184.

3. Higgs, Liz Curtis, *Mad Mary: A Bad Girl from Magdala, Transformed at His Appearing* (Colorado Springs, CO: WaterBrook Press, 2001), 260.

4. Strobel, Lee, *The Case for Easter: A Journalist Investigates the Evidence for the Resurrection* (Grand Rapids, MI: Zondervan, 1998), 25.

5. Haidle, Helen, *Journey to the Cross: The Complete Easter Story for Young Readers* (Grand Rapids, MI: Zonderkidz, 2001), 183, Conclusion.

6. Maier, 198.

7. Geisler, Norman L., *The Battle for the Resurrection* (Nashville, TN: Thomas Nelson, 1989).

8. House, H. Wayne, *Chronological and Background Charts of the New Testament* (Grand Rapids, MI: Zondervan, 1981), 133.

9. Maier, 188.

Strobel, *The Case for Christ: A Journalist's Personal Investigation of the Evidence for Jesus* (Grand Rapids, MI: Zondervan, 1998), 72.

Geisler, 141.

10. Geisler, 141.

11. Moore, Beth, *Beloved Disciple: The Life and Ministry of John* (Nashville, TN: LifeWay Press, 2002), 65-66.

"Overview of the Spring Holidays," http://biblicalholidays.com.

Ray Vander Laan and Focus on the Family Video, *The True Easter Story, That the World May Know* (Grand Rapids, MI: Zondervan, 2000).

12. *The Narrated Bible in Chronological Order*, F. LaGard Smith, (Eugene, Oregon: Harvest House, 1984), 1488

13. Morison, Frank, *Who Moved the Stone? A Skeptic Looks at the Death and Resurrection of Christ* (Grand Rapids, MI: Zondervan, 1930), 115.

14. Osbeck, Kenneth, *Amazing Grace 366 Inspiring Hymn Stories for Daily Devotions*, (Grand Rapids, Michigan: Kregel, 1990), 112.

Hymn Research:

Emurian, Ernest K., *Famous Stories of Inspiring Hymns* (Grand Rapids, MI: Kregel, 1956).

———, *Hymn Stories for Programs* (Grand Rapids, MI: Baker Book House, 1963).

Osbeck, Kenneth W., *Amazing Grace: 366 Inspiring Hymn Stories for Daily Devotions* (Grand Rapids, MI: Kregel, 1990).

———, *101 Hymn Stories: The Inspiring True Stories Behind 101 Favorite Hymns* (Grand Rapids, MI: Kregel, 1982).

Bailey, Albert Edward: *The Gospel in Hymns: Background and Interpretation* (New York: Charles Scribner's Sons: 1950).

Preparing My Heart for Easter
Guide for Leaders

Other materials and resources to consider:

DVD: Ray Vander Laan's *The True Easter Story: The Promise Kept.* I strongly encourage the purchase of this inexpensive and beautiful video from Focus on the Family and That the World May Know Ministries. I also highly recommend any DVD in the "That the World May Know" video series. Check to see if your church library has this resource.

Handel's *Messiah* (Easter portion)

Easter music CD's

Devotions for Lent

Scenes from movies depicting the life, death, or resurrection of Jesus

The Visual Bible (http://www.visualbible.com): *Jesus The Christ, Matthew, Falling Fire*

Jesus, directed by Sykes, Kirsh

Ask members to share Easter resources.

See the endnotes for additional resources.

Preview—Conduct a meeting prior to Ash Wednesday

Discuss:

What do you remember about past Easters?

What made certain Easters more memorable?

What would your ideal Easter be like?

How do you want this Easter to be different?

Pass out the study and introduce the format.

Show: *The True Easter Story: The Promise Kept* (That the World May Know series)

Music: Play selections from Handel's *Messiah*—The Easter portion as members enter.

Connections: Ask members to sign an information sheet. Prepare a list of names, addresses, phone numbers and E-mails. Ask members to bring in their personal Easter resources to share.

WEEK ONE: PREPARING FOR THE JOURNEY—AFTER FIRST FIVE DAYS OF STUDY

Discuss:

Each week select questions for your group and ask members to share questions, reflections, and new learning.

1. Why is Easter sometimes given less importance than Christmas?
2. How could Easter be much more?
3. How have you celebrated the Lenten season in the past?
4. How have members celebrated Ash Wednesday?
5. Where are you on the spectrum of Women?
6. What would have attracted you to Jesus?
7. What surprised you about how Jesus included women in His storytelling?
8. What surprised you about women of AD 30?
9. What did you learn about "I AM" statements?

Show: *Life and Ministry of the Messiah—The Rabbi* (That the World May Know series)

Music: "Near the Cross," "Hallelujah What a Savior," "Tell Me the Stories of Jesus"

Preview: Traveling with Jesus: Five Women Touched by Him

Connections: Pass out list of addresses. Pass out a 3 x 5 card to each woman and ask them to write down their hopes for spiritual growth this Easter. Take the cards and pray for the women. Contact each one of them with a note card.

Memorize: John 13:34 or John 14:6

WEEK TWO: TRAVELING WITH JESUS— FIVE WOMEN TOUCHED BY HIM

Discuss:

1. When is your quiet time?" Re: "In the morning"
2. Any new understanding about women of the N.T.?
3. How are these encounters obviously not accidents?
4. How did Jesus meet you?
5. How is it reassuring to know that Jesus is the Great I Am?
6. What is one "takeaway" you learned from Jesus' encounter with each of the women this week? (Mother-in-law, Samaritan, adulterous woman, widow, sinner woman, Mary Magdalene)

Show: *Death and Resurrection: Piercing the Darkness* (That the World May Know series)

Music: "What Wondrous Love Is This?" "I am Thine O Lord"

Preview: Traveling with Jesus—Six Women Touched by Him

Connections: Pass out 3x5 note cards and ask each woman to write down a current prayer request. Have the women exchange cards with one another and place their friend's card in their Bible to keep their person in prayer.

Memorize: John 7:38–39 or Psalm 34:18

WEEK THREE: TRAVELING WITH JESUS— SIX WOMEN TOUCHED BY HIM

Discuss:

1. What is one "takeaway" you learned from Jesus' encounter with each of the women this week? (Jairus' daughter, hemorrhaging woman, Canaanite mother, Mary and Martha, bent woman, Salome)

2. When you see a familiar story to "restudy," how do you approach it so it is fresh (for example, Mary and Martha)?

3. Which of these characters were unfamiliar to you?

4. Which of the characters were familiar but taught you something new? What was the new concept you learned?

Music: "And Can It Be That I Should Gain," "My Jesus I Love Thee"

Preview: Jesus Enters Jerusalem—An Overview of the Last Week

Connections: Pass out 3x5 cards and ask each woman to put their name and contact information on it. Mix up the cards and pass them out so each woman has a person to contact over the next week through a cheerful uplifting phone call, e-mail, or snail mail.

Memorize: John 11:25–26, Romans 12:1–2

WEEK FOUR: JESUS ENTERS JERUSALEM— AN OVERVIEW OF THE LAST WEEK

Discuss:

1. Which Gospel writer spoke to you this week?

2. Which stories popped out to you as new or unfamiliar?

3. What differences did you notice in the treatments?

4. What lessons seemed specifically from Jesus to YOU?

Show: *The True Easter Story: The Promise Kept* (That the World May Know series; if you did not show it at a preview meeting)

Music: "The Old Rugged Cross," "There is a Fountain Filled with Blood," "Nothing but the Blood"

Preview: Passion Week—Increasing Tension

Connections: Pass out 3x5 cards and ask each woman to write down a special verse from the past week's lesson. Swap cards with one another.

Memorize: Luke 9:23

WEEK FIVE: PASSION WEEK— INCREASING TENSION

Discuss:

1. What surprised you from this week's lesson?
2. How is God working in your life this Lent season?
3. How will you celebrate Easter differently this year?
4. If you were in Jerusalem at the time, where would you be physically and spiritually?
5. What kind of king are you looking for?
6. What surprised you about the Q and A sessions from Wednesday?
7. Which of Thursday's *Last Lessons* did you study and what did you learn?
8. What does it mean to live out Matthew 16:24?

Show: *The True Easter Story—Lamb of God* (That the World May Know series)

Music: "How Beautiful," "Lamb of God," "You are my All in All," "There is a Redeemer"

Preview: Passion Week—The Last Days

Connections: Bring red construction paper hearts jaggedly cut or torn in half. Pass out one half of a heart to each woman and have her write down her name and a prayer request on that piece. Ask each woman to find the match to her broken heart. Discuss how the women we've studied hearts must have been breaking and that Jesus mends broken hearts. Ask each member to contact her "match" during the week.

Memorize: Zechariah 9:9 or Psalm 118:22–23 or John 12:24–25

WEEK SIX: PASSION WEEK— THE LAST DAYS

Discuss:

1. How do you see God's love revealed through the Passion of Jesus?
2. What do the symbols of Easter represent to you?
3. What do you learn from the marriage analogy Christ uses?
4. Which of Jesus' final teachings were significant to you this week?
5. What look does Jesus give you?
6. The group could reenact a Passover service.
7. The leader could wash the feet of the women in the group

Show: *Death and Resurrection: The Weight of the World* (That the World May Know series)

Music: "O Sacred Head," "When I Survey the Wondrous Cross," "Hosanna, Loud Hosanna!"

Preview: <u>Death and Resurrection</u>

Connections: Pass out a sheet of paper to each member, then go around the room and trace each member's foot on the sheet. Then ask each woman to write down an area where she needs to walk like Jesus and serve. Each member should take home their foot as a visual reminder to step out in loving service.

Memorize: Mark 10:45, or John 14:5–7, or John 16:33

WEEK SEVEN:
DEATH AND RESURRECTION

Triduum: Maundy Thursday, Good Friday, The Great Vigil

Discuss:

1.   Consider the Ash Wednesday practice of marking the forehead with ashes. Ask each member to wipe off the mark and carry the inward remembrance that Jesus took away our sins.

2.   Consider celebrating the Lord' Supper and washing one another's feet.

3.   Discuss ways we can show we are Christians by our love.

4.   Consider reading through the Last Words of Jesus and extinguishing candles during the remembrance.

5.   Consider having dramatic readings using scenes from Gethsemane to Golgotha

6.   Why does Easter give you hope?

7.   What's different about this Easter?

Music: "Jesus Christ is Risen Today," "Christ the Lord is Risen Today"

Show: *Death and Resurrection—Roll Away the Stone* (That the World May Know series)

Preview: <u>Where Do We Go from Here?</u>

Connections: Pass out a rock and felt permanent marker to each woman. Ask her to write down a hope she has for her Christian walk, a longstanding prayer, or something she longs to see resurrected in her life. This is a paperweight and a reminder that no stone is too big for God.

Memorize: Galatians 6:14 or John 15:10–11 or John 5:24

Can you think of a time when you had mixed emotions about what God told you to do? How did you handle that?

WEEK EIGHT: WHERE DO WE GO FROM HERE?

Discuss:

1. How do you feel when someone uses *your* name?
2. What role does the Holy Spirit play in your life?
3. What does the blood, the cross, and discipleship mean to you now?
4. What is your level of commitment to Jesus now? Why?
5. Using Week One's list of women, who do you now relate to most?
6. Where do we go from here? (group or personal studies)

Music: "Are You Washed in the Blood?" or "Rejoice the Lord is King!"

Show: *Life and Ministry of Messiah—No Greater Love* (That the World May Know series)

Death and Resurrection—Power to the People (That the World May Know series)

Connections: Share answers to prayer you've experienced, and ask for additional prayer requests. Ask each member to continue praying for the others in the group.

Memorize: 1 Peter 2:24 or 1 John 1:7